PRAISE FROM READ
Majoring in the Rest of Your Life

I think your book is GREAT!

It really puts everything in perspective. Instead of looking at college as many hazy years in front of me, I now have a "game plan" from which to work. —JULIE M. STREUFERT, Deer Lodge, Montana

This book has had a *major* influence on my life!

I think *Majoring* should be required reading for *every* college student! —TAMMY LEARY, Arvada, Colorado

Your book has gotten me very excited about my future.

I will recommend it to my friends and schoolmates in the hope that it will be as beneficial to them as it has been, and will continue to be, to me. —HILARY M. LAWN, Palm Harbor, Florida

PRAISE FOR
Graduating into the Nineties

A very upbeat and useful guide for new job hunters. —MARY FAN KAIN, assistant director, Office of Career Services, Harvard University

Every newly employed graduate should have a copy. —BARBARA HAMILTON, PH.D., director, Freshman Rhetoric Program, Oakland University, Michigan

DISCARD

MAJORING
IN
HIGH
SCHOOL

Survival Tips for Students

CAROL
CARTER

THE NOONDAY PRESS
Farrar, Straus and Giroux
New York

Copyright © 1995 by Carol Carter
Published simultaneously in Canada by HarperCollins*CanadaLtd*
Printed in the United States of America
First edition, 1995

LIBRARY OF CONGRESS CATALOGING-IN-PUBLICATION DATA
Carter, Carol.
Majoring in high school : survival tips for students /
Carol Carter. — 1st ed.
p.   cm.
1. High school students—Psychology.   2. Self-actualization
(Psychology).   3. Self-realization.   4. Vocational guidance.
I. Title.
LB1620.C37   1995   373.18—dc20   94-41603   CIP

TO BILL CLEMENTS

Who dedicated himself to the education and achievement of all students throughout their lives and who understood—because he himself had realized—the power of human potential.

For your spirit, your energy, your determination, your time, your interest, and your ever-present leadership and counsel, this one is for you.

ACKNOWLEDGMENTS

There are a lot of people whose time, energy, and creative talent went into this book.

First, the people in LifeSkills, a nonprofit organization serving high school students in New York City and Tucson, Arizona, saw a need for a book that really addressed the concerns and issues of today's high school students. LifeSkills provides a program that combines a course of reading and exercises with exposure to a variety of community members and businesspeople. Together, these two elements provide students with a realistic composite view of what it takes to succeed in today's workplace. Executive Director of the Tucson program Shirley Kiser, her administrative assistant Helen Marty and program coordinator Dorothy Steele, and the New York program's Program Director John Torrente and Co-ordinator of Program Development Judy Kallick Russell have combined their energies to continue to expand the scope and the power of LifeSkills. They helped me to conceive a book that conveys the basics of high school survival while encouraging the students, through real-life examples and stories, to reach for their dream career goals.

Second, my brother Kent and I brainstormed what such a book could be like. Kent went home and four weeks later mailed me his ideas for a manuscript that included opening each chapter by featuring someone from history, literature, or contemporary life whom the students would know or might learn about during high school. His insight and thoughtful perspective shaped the core of this book. We kept thinking through the best ways to connect to students while dredging up many of our own high school experiences.

Third, Sarah Lyman Kravits, Anne Riddick, and Cynthia Nordberg interviewed current and former students about their experiences both in school and out. Thanks, too, to Virginia Stanek at Sunnyside High School in Tucson and Isabelle Fitzgerald at Manhattan Comprehensive

Night High School in New York, two teachers who gathered stories from their students for the book. We also worked with Ted Wallin and Brad Miller at Syracuse University to capture the high school experiences of college freshmen while the stories were still vivid in their memories. Special thanks go to Sarah Lyman Kravits, who is my partner, my inspiration, my athletic companion, and one of my closest friends. Her special approach to life—and her passion for anything she undertakes—makes being with her and working with her rewarding and enjoyable. Sarah, here's to working together into *our* nineties!

Finally, we received feedback from and would like to thank Judy Bowers, Vicki Saxon, Shirley Kiser, and Madeline Beita, all present or former teachers or counselors. After numerous phone calls and revisions, final changes were made.

As always, my family and friends have been supportive and encouraging of this and each of the books I have written. Their faith and constant love have enabled me to make the most of what I have experienced in my life.

Last but not least, my editor Elisabeth Kallick Dyssegaard has continually supported achievement for students of all ages. Her ability to focus Farrar, Straus and Giroux on issues that affect students has opened up a world of possibilities for me to communicate my message and vision for students.

I also need to thank the board members of the two branches of LifeSkills, whose efforts have helped my ideas find fertile ground:

In New York: Funmi Arewa, Sherry Bloomberg, Jerry Callaghan, Ken Elgarten, Rama Moorthy, Wayne Olson, Pernell Parker, Jonathan Schorr, and Lynn Troyka.

In Tucson: Edna Meza Aguirre, Jim Barnyak, Fred Bull, Bill Clements, Dr. Pedro Delgado, Steve Johnson, Jana Kooi, Francine Rienstra, Kent Rollins, Jordan Simon, Robert A. Strauss, and Dr. John Taylor.

And finally, a special thank-you to all of the students, former students, and working people listed below who volunteered their personal stories for this book. Your experiences, insight, and lessons learned will reach many who can benefit from your wisdom.

Gilbert Aguilar	Rus Blackwell	Tom Burdasz
Becky Amato	Heather Bliss	Kathryn Byrnes
Dan Austin	Chet Bloom	Nicole Caplan
Clifford Balanag	Paula Bobrowski	Frank Caporrino
Angela Baldwin	Gail Brown	Gavin Carrier
Sara Banker	Kimberly Buckley	Dave Case
Elissa Barnes	Tracy Green Bunch	Michael Cellucci

Carrie Chapman
Dominic Ciresi
Maureen Clancy
Eileen Cook
Shaun Crawford
Nelson Cruz
Sarah Czeladnicki
Brooke Davis
Eric Davis
Maggie Debelius
Kimberly Diamond
Angela Dorn
Joanne Ebeling
Bryce Edwards
Dale Ellis
Rex Randall Erickson
Alex Estrella
James Favicchio
Laurie Fuentes
Judith Goodman
Dustin Grimm
Kristina Hahn
Faraz Haider
Kelly Hines
Michael Hobler
Jeffrey Hoffman
Lisa Ivy
Kirk Jennings
Jeremy Kaber
Bryan Kenny
David Kobin
Jason Kovar
Garth Kravits

Sarah Lyman Kravits
Amanda Lee
Joon Lee
Rebecca Lemberger
Tamika Leslie
Jim Lindsey
Maria Lopez
Mira Lowenthal
Sandra McCullough
Connie McGuire
Tanaphon Manavutiveth
Cyrus Massoumi
Justin Meitzer
Daneka Mocarski
Lydia Molina
Tiffany Moncrieffe
James Morris
Deena Mottola
Edison Munizaga
Carol Mylovsky
Michael Nahum
Cynthia Nordberg
Katy O'Connor
Holmes Osborne
Mitchell Polack
Heather Pollack
Lee Pomeroy
Raquel Ramirez
Melissa Rekas
Donny Reyes
Patrice Richards
Jessica Riese
Melissa Romero

David Rowe
Sharifah Sams
Eve Sangenito
Shirley Saylor
Mikah Don Sellers
Andrea Smalling
Joseph Smith
Jackie Spence
Floris Suarez
John Torrente
Sara Verhey
Miroslav Vucetic
Annie Wagner
Ryan Walker
Andy Wardlaw
Patrick Weisel
Joshua Weissman
Christy Wells
Gwenan Wilbur
Susan Winchester
William Wolfe
Paul Youkilis
Jeannine Young
Jeff Zimon
John Zora

Many, many thanks for opening up your lives and passing on your legacy of knowledge.

CONTENTS

FOREWORD BY LES BROWN   XV
WHY I WROTE THIS BOOK   3

PART ONE: **KNOWING YOURSELF**

1   BEING A TEENAGER
    Where You're At Right Now   7

    • Factors in Your World   8
        Tough Environments   8
        Hormones Gone Crazy   10
        Self-absorption   10
    • Living with High School   13
        Academic Issues   13
        Social Issues   15
        Responsibility   17
        Fears   20
    • What Is the Point of High School?   22
    • What Do You Have to Offer?   23

2   GETTING ADJUSTED
    Figuring Yourself Out   25

    • *Close Up:* William Butler Yeats, Poet   25
    • Discovering Yourself   26
        Your Environment   27
        What You Do   28
        How You Relate to Others   30
    • Interests and Talents   32
        Take Your Time   33
        Take Your Own Personal Inventory   34

Keep Learning about Yourself   38
• Finding Confidence   39
Give It Time   42

3   REACHING OUT
Your Relationships with Others   43

• *Close Up:* Dorothy Reed Mendenhall, Physician   43
• Relating to the People in Your Life   44
Friends   45
Family   49
Teachers and Other Authority Figures   51
Boyfriends and Girlfriends: To Date or Not to Date   54
The Diverse World: Dealing with Differences   58

4   UNCOVERING OPPORTUNITIES
Education Inside and Outside the Classroom   62

• *Close Up:* Miles Davis, Jazz Musician   62
• Areas of Educational Opportunity   63
School   63
Extracurricular Activities   66
Working Part-time   70
Internships and Co-ops   72
• Human Resources   73
Counselors and Advisers   74
Role Models   75
Mentors   76

PART TWO: EXPLORING YOUR WORLD

5   BALANCING YOUR PRIORITIES AND SETTING GOALS
Identifying What You Want and Planning How to Get It   83

• *Close Up:* Dave Winfield, Baseball Player   83
• Defining Your Values   84
• Goal-setting   91
Envisioning Your Goals   92
Working toward Your Goals   93
Reassessing and Modifying Your Goals   98
• Priorities   100
• Juggling Your Priorities: Time Management   103

6 BECOMING MOTIVATED
What You'll Need to Move Ahead 108

- *Close Up:* Margaret Mead, Anthropologist 108
- Attitude 109
- Initiative 112
- Decision-making 114
- Motivation 121
- Commitment 123

7 TAKING CARE OF YOURSELF
Staying Healthy and Happy Inside and Out 127

- *Close Up:* Jane Addams, Social Worker 127
- Physical Health 128
- Mental Health 131
  Managing Stress 131
  Finding the Fun 136
- Alcohol, Cigarettes, and Drugs 138
- Sexual Issues 144

PART THREE: EXPANDING YOUR WORLD

8 GETTING HIRED, GETTING ACCEPTED
Applying for Jobs and to Colleges 151

- *Close Up:* Winston Churchill, Statesman 151
- Making Plans That Fit You 152
- Information Gathering 155
  Written Resources 156
  Networking: The Human Resource 157
- Job Applications 161
  Applications 161
  Résumés 164
  Cover Letters 168
  Interviews 168
- College Applications and Interviews 174
- Success and Failure 177

9 OPENING DOORS
Joining the Academic and Working Worlds 181

- *Close Up:* Charlayne Hunter-Gault, Journalist/News
  Correspondent 181

• Making the Transition   183
    Workplace   184
    College   186
• Social Politics   189
    Workplace   190
    College   191
• Street Smarts   192
    Workplace   194
    College   195
• Your Rights on the Job or at School   195
    Treatment   195
    Feedback   198
    Paperwork   198
    Additional Rights on the Job   198
    Additional Rights at College   198
• Focusing on the Big Picture: Lifelong Learning   199
• The Difference You Make   201

AFTERWORD   203

APPENDIXES

A   Suggested Reading   207
B   Clubs and Group Activities   212
C   Scholarships, Awards, Grants, and Loans   218

FOREWORD

My twin brother and I were born on a floor in low-income Liberty City in Miami, Florida, and were adopted at six weeks old by Mrs. Mamie Brown, a single woman who had very little education and financial means but a very big heart. She believed in me and encouraged me all during her lifetime.

School was a different story. I was labeled "educable mentally retarded" in elementary school. In high school, a very special teacher, Leroy Washington, taught me to respect myself and not believe what others said about my abilities. He convinced me to go after my dreams through self-education. I have never had a formal day of college, but since that time I have been committed to becoming educated—a process that will continue forever. I read constantly, attend lectures, and communicate with people of all backgrounds on all kinds of subjects.

I hope this book will be for you what my high school teacher was for me: a reason to get out of the ordinary and the everyday so that you can achieve your greatness and know what is special within yourself and work hard to develop those qualities in your mind and in your heart. Whether you go to college, to vocational school, or into the workplace after high school, make a commitment to lifelong learning. It will give you the competitive edge in any career or business, and it will create a deeper awareness of what is meaningful in life.

So go after your dreams. Don't settle for anything less. Reading *Majoring in High School* will start you on that path to your success, but you are the one who determines the extent to which you can achieve your limitless potential. You have greatness within you!

—Les Brown

MAJORING
IN
HIGH
SCHOOL

WHY I WROTE THIS BOOK

I was about the most uninterested, disconnected teenager you ever met. I had no idea of who I was or where my life was going. All I knew was that high school was what everybody did for at least a period of time until they dropped out or graduated, and then went to college or got a job. I figured I wasn't going to drop out, but I didn't believe I could excel. I didn't even have the desire to do well because I didn't really understand how this high school experience was going to relate to the rest of my life. I saw it as an opportunity to pass the time. Just show up, I thought, and things will take care of themselves.

Then the alarm clock of life went off in my brain. It was set off by one of my brothers, who gave me the greatest jolt and the greatest gift of my life: a reality check.

Craig taught me these hard lessons about high school and life in general:

1. You can't just show up in life and expect things to happen. You have to go after what you want and make it happen.
2. People who are bored with life haven't discovered what is special about them—what inspires and energizes them more than anything else. Discovering this in yourself—whether your passion is theater, football, painting, chemistry, swimming, home decorating, welding, stand-up comedy—is one of the first steps to pursuing a rewarding career. It is one of the things that make life meaningful.
3. High school is one of the best places to get a well-rounded education. Whether you decide to go to a vocational school, to college, or straight into the work force, you will always need the tool that is your brain. If you use your time in high school to learn new skills, keep informed about what is happening in the world around

you, and maintain a general interest in learning, you will be ahead of the pack when you leave.

It was too bad that I didn't learn these lessons until my senior year of high school—at that point, I had wasted a lot of valuable time. Fortunately, Craig's advice and words of wisdom from my other brothers really caused me to get my act together before beginning college. I worked my tail off in college to make up for my high school years. It was worth it. I earned a great education, and I was able to get a really rewarding job when I graduated.

This book is intended to give you the survival and success secrets that high school students need to know but are seldom told. In it I raise important issues and give you advice so that you can think things through and make the best decisions for yourself. Most of all, I hope this book helps you to unlock all of the human potential and greatness that is within you. HAVE NO FEAR! Go after your dreams and make them happen.

PART ONE

KNOWING YOURSELF

BEING A TEENAGER
Where You're At Right Now

A s I interviewed scores of students and former students for this book, and as I thought about my own experience in high school, I began to see that there are two universal truths about being a teenager that make just as much sense today as they did a hundred years ago:

Everybody is unique, different, and special.
Nobody has it easy.

Teenagers face all kinds of different challenges, from everyday have-tos to decisions that could change the course of a life. Christy Wells, a high school student in Tucson, Arizona, had to deal with the question of parenthood. "Just over a year ago, I had to make the most important decision of my life—the decision between abortion, adoption, and keeping the young life that was growing inside me. I was only sixteen when I found out I was pregnant, a sophomore in high school. My whole future lay ahead of me. I was scared and didn't know what to do. Finally I came to the decision (with the father's help) to keep the child. This meant a whole new life for the father and me. Now I am eighteen, and my daughter is one and a half. I am in my senior year, preparing to graduate. I go to four classes a day and work for the County Recorders the rest of the day."

Lee Pomeroy, a journalist in Chicago, remembers the awkwardness of an unfamiliar environment. "Very early in high school, I had the opportunity to be an exchange student in Sweden. I was frightened at first because I was shy, and I didn't think the family I was living with would like me. There were language barriers, and at the outset I was very lonely. Eventually I became close to the family and learned a lot from my experiences. The most important thing I realized was that Cincinnati, Ohio, was not the cultural norm for the entire world."

David Rowe, now an art historian, had to wait until college before he learned something about himself that had given him trouble at St.

Ignatius High School in Chicago. "The high school I attended had an excellent reputation and brought in high-achieving students from all over the area. Unfortunately, I was never more than an average student. No matter how hard I tried, the best I could do was swing B's and C's. This was very difficult for me as a middle-class African-American male because the peer pressure was really on to do well and prove myself. There was a great deal of competition. None of the academic subjects I needed to pursue the 'in' professions (medicine, law, business) interested me, and I ended up doing just the bare minimum to get through. In college I was tested, and it turned out that I have a learning disability. Discovering that I learn best by association and visual stimulation helped me find art history—a subject I loved."

Everyone has a story to tell. No matter how together they seem, most people have had to deal with tough circumstances at some point or other, and chances are that some of their most challenging times came during their teen years. Why? Because as a teenager you are in the most transitional time of your life. You were a child for twelve years. Your challenge now is to develop into an adult—a physically, emotionally, and intellectually mature person who may have to make decisions about jobs, college, and even marriage and family. You have many years ahead to *be* an adult, and only a very short time to make the transition. It's a lot to expect of anyone. It's hard to grow up when you have to spend so much time figuring out who you are and where you fit in—discovering yourself is, after all, your most consuming activity right now. But it's something everyone has to face.

Factors in Your World

My own growing-up process revealed to me three factors that shape the teen experience and lead all of us along our separate paths to adulthood: *Environment, Hormones,* and a capacity for *Self-absorption.* Everyone has to cope with these, and no one has any real control over them. I had very powerful experiences with each and have come to see how they helped create who I am today. If you understand these forces in your life, you can learn how to find their positive sides, and eventually you might be able to use them to your benefit.

Tough Environments

When I first started high school, I felt awkward, self-conscious, and full of anxiety about what lay ahead. I was raised in a house with four older brothers. Each of them was accomplished and talented in some way that made me, as I compared myself to them, feel very *unaccomplished*. What made matters worse was that my brothers were highly critical of me (maybe my parents had been harsh to them). They were always pointing out to me how clueless I was about things and pushing me to do what they thought I should. My usual reaction was to pull away, to give up, to quit before I even started to try. As I saw it, my family was hard on me, and it made me an uninterested, disconnected teenager who didn't know where she fit in.

Perhaps you are from some sort of tough environment yourself. Maybe your parents are divorced. Maybe you are being raised by a single parent who has to work so hard to support you financially that there isn't a lot of emotional support coming your way. Maybe your parents show their love for you with material objects or discipline rather than time spent together. Perhaps you have been abused in some way—physically or emotionally—that affects how you feel about yourself.

Keep two things in mind about the condition of your environment. First, almost everybody has to cope with tough family situations in some shape or form. You are not alone! In fact, I don't know anybody who hasn't had some set of family problems affect them as a teenager. I have one friend whose parents divorced and whose mother married a control freak who would blow up at my friend if she so much as left an empty glass on the counter. Another acquaintance, while still a sophomore, lost his father to a heart attack. A third encountered unrelenting pressure from her parents to surpass everyone else in her class. Even seemingly harmless teasing from a sibling, or having to come home to an empty house every day after school, has its effect.

Second, no matter how trapped you may feel at the moment, you have the power to climb up and away from your circumstances so that they don't hold you back and prevent you from achieving your dreams. Sometimes it takes a long time for us to understand our basic fears and anxieties. Some people's emotional trauma—from a critical parent, harsh siblings, or other situations—can be just as hard to overcome as physical limitations. Almost all people, when they are honest with themselves, can find some circumstance or event in their teenage years that was, or is, a disadvantage and potentially disabling factor if not handled properly. That's the difficult part of life. But the silver lining is knowing that no matter what limits you, you have the ability to deal with it and improve the other things about yourself over which you have more control. Your experiences can be not only bearable but useful as you develop your knowledge and talents through these years.

Hormones Gone Crazy

The teen years are a time when human bodies undergo tremendous change. As you develop into a young adult, what goes on with your hormones—and your whole system—can make you angry, sad, un-interested, and detached from what is happening around you. You need time to get used to the new and strong mix of hormones that are roaming around your body, and making the adjustment can cause you to experience wide swings of emotion. You may feel extraordinarily happy or overwhelmingly depressed over what someone else might think is nothing at all. You may find yourself thinking obsessively about one event, subject, or person for long periods of time. You may angrily overreact to what friends, parents, and siblings do or say. THIS IS NORMAL. Although it is not always fun to go through, it helps to know that there is a rational biological reason for your sometimes ir-rational feelings.

I still have my journal from this time in my life. There were days when I felt so down and so lonely that my connection to the world seemed quite remote. I drew pictures in my journal of myself during this time—and they were scary-looking! My emotional swings centered on whether or not my crush *du jour* was interested in me. If he was, my heart soared; if not, I was thrown into the depths of despair.

Sarah Lyman Kravits, an actor and writer living in New York City, wrote a few "scary" things in her journal as well. "I went back recently and looked at my journal from freshman year of high school, when I had become overwhelmingly aware of myself and my shortcomings. Whenever anything went wrong in my life, it acted as a trigger that reminded me of every other reason why I should be depressed. One particularly awful day, I closed my door, lay on my bed in misery, and filled ten pages with a list of everything that was wrong with me and my life, everything from 'my feet are too big' to 'so-and-so didn't look at me when I passed his locker' and even 'none of my friends really care about me anyway because no one invited me over this week and no one passed me any notes.' " The littlest things mean so much!

Self-absorption

Most of what you're going through now involves focusing on you. That's okay, because in order to learn about something so mysterious and complex as yourself, you need to spend a lot of time and energy focusing inward. But this can result in having difficulty staying sensitive to the needs of the people around you. Many teenagers have to work extra hard to maintain some focus outside the self; some succeed, and some don't.

Since this time is so emotionally charged, you have a greater capacity to be not only harsh on yourself but harsh with others as well. Teenagers can be mean! You may know this from either bearing the brunt of cruelty or being the cause of it—most people experience both sides of the coin. Emotions run so high that it can be hard to contain them; and when they are let loose, nasty things can happen. I remember one particularly bad fight I had with my mother. Our fight ended in a shouting match and I yelled, "I hate you," and left the room. I went into my room and cried, and I immediately began to feel terrible about telling my mom, whom I really did love, that I hated her. I knew I must have hurt her. A few hours later, my mom came into my room, her eyes red from crying. I apologized, and we both had a good cry together.

I know now that if I had possessed the ability to turn my focus outward and notice my mother's needs and troubles, I might have been able to control my anger better. Years later I found out that my mom was dealing with a lot of other pressures at that time that I knew nothing about—financial worries, my dad's illness, and her own experience with menopause. In my self-absorption, I was not yet able to understand my mother's needs, so I let my feelings out before I thought about how they would affect her.

Jim Lindsey, a college graduate who is working for a temporary service in Washington, D.C., ended up on the receiving end of some typical cruelty. "There were two really sharp guys in high school who teamed up on me and verbally tormented me. They were very quick-witted. I wasn't quick enough to get them back, and I wasn't together enough to ignore it. So I would just let their teasing eat away at me. It is really awful that one or two people can have the power to make your teen years miserable. Looking back now, I see the best thing to have done would have been to walk away from people like that, and I wasn't ever able to do that completely. The thing you learn as you get older is that kids can be cruel sometimes and that although adults can be cruel as well, they have more social restraints on them. As an adult, you learn to let it roll off and not let it control your life. You realize it is someone else's insecurity causing them to act that way."

During my senior year of high school, my brother Craig helped me begin to focus on the world outside of myself. He took time to investigate what was going on with me. On a holiday break from his college, he cornered me and started to ask me a lot of questions about what I wanted to do with my life, what interested me, what I thought about all day. I said "I don't know" to just about every question, which frustrated him. He began criticizing my constant talking on the phone and going to concerts instead of studying. He said if I approached work or college in the same uninterested way that I approached high school, I would be spending the rest of my life flipping burgers. He told me to quit making excuses, decide what I wanted out of life, and begin planning how to achieve it, or I would waste my talents and my brains.

Well, the ball was in my court, but I didn't like it. I wanted to be on the sidelines. How dare he interfere with my life and make me feel so awful about myself! What I realized later was that much of my anger came from being scared that he was right. I did want to be "somebody" and make a difference, I realized, but I wasn't sure how, because I had never tried before.

Although I wouldn't speak to Craig, I started acting on what he had said. I went to the library and checked out six books that I had heard were "classics," ones that I hadn't been assigned in class: *Pride and Prejudice* by Jane Austen, *The Great Gatsby* by F. Scott Fitzgerald, *For Whom the Bell Tolls* and *A Farewell to Arms* by Ernest Hemingway, *A Portrait of the Artist as a Young Man* by James Joyce, and *Sister Carrie* by Theodore Dreiser. I made an effort to work harder in school and improved my grades in my last semester. I started reading newspapers and tried to include *Time* magazine with my *Vogue*s and *Mademoiselle*s. Slowly I discovered that there were many things I enjoyed about learning—I liked knowing about things, I liked being able to discuss them with other people and feel as if I could hold my own, and I actually liked feeling more on top of my work at school.

My brother and I didn't remain angry at each other for long. He wrote me from college and let me know that although he hadn't really enjoyed talking to me that way, he felt he needed to do it because he cared about me and my future. To this day I have continually turned to him for help and advice. He made a difference in my life because he showed me how to believe in myself. He let me know that I mattered and that I had unique talents to offer the world, even if I didn't know what they were yet. He also let me know that he believed in me, and that kind of support still helps me keep going in those times when I doubt myself. Everyone can benefit from someone like Craig—someone who takes a special interest.

Living with High School

You're dealing with a lot right now. High school catapults you into a new world both academically and socially, and both areas offer you good things as well as problems that get on your nerves.

Academic Issues

Pressure to do well in your classes, dealing with homework, figuring out which teachers you click with and which you are uninspired by or actively dislike, overworking yourself, or finding yourself bored with your classes—all these issues come up from time to time. Even getting adjusted to the high school environment takes some doing. When you move into high school, you enter a world unlike any you have ever known. I was overwhelmed by my first taste of it. One of the reasons getting adjusted was so hard for me is that I came from a small private school. In eighth grade, there were only twelve students in my class. My public high school, by contrast, had more than 2,000 students— 640 in the freshman class alone. I felt lost at first, like a kid at Disney World who couldn't find her parents. It was intimidating and frightening.

I'll never forget the sound of the bell ringing at 7:50 a.m. on my first day of high school. I had ten minutes to get to the right room, but I was terrified that I wouldn't make it. I remember looking at the room number on my schedule three or more times as I made my way nervously up a flight of stairs, concerned every step of the way that I was going to end up in the wrong room and that people would laugh and tease me. Finally I found the room and made it to an empty chair without tripping over myself. The teacher called off the roll, and I breathed a sigh of relief when I heard my name. I knew I was in the right place, if nothing else. But that was only the first crisis I faced— as I looked around at the sea of faces in what was the largest classroom I had ever been in, I realized that I didn't know a single person. The other students all seemed to know one another, and I felt totally alone.

Despite my apprehensions, I made it through the first day of school and, before I knew it, the first week. It took a while for me to feel secure in my new environment. But by the end of my freshman year, I realized that getting adjusted to high school was similar to other new beginnings I had already faced in my life. At one time, my old school had also been a new and unfamiliar place. Knowing I had made successful adjustments before helped me understand and face the new situation. Recalling experiences in your past often allows you to tackle a new challenge with greater confidence.

Sometimes people move down more difficult paths to reach a place of comfort in high school. Laurie Fuentes, a high school junior in Tucson, found herself avoiding high school before she could accept it. "When I had just turned thirteen, I moved from living in Hawaii with my mom to living with my grandparents in Arizona, in a strange city with a totally different environment. But I needed a secure, loving home, and I knew I could have it with my grandparents. It was hard adjusting to a new school for the first time in my life. At first I kept to myself and missed as many days of school as possible. I had a tough time conforming to the rules and ways of my new family. Now I realize how much they put up with me. I think the past five years have taught me so much about life and made me a stronger person. So when I graduate, I know that even though it took me five years to adjust, I've come a long way."

Some of you might feel that high school is boring or a waste of your time. You may not be quite sure why you have to go through all the classes, why you should care about the activities, why you should take time to get to know teachers and people outside your normal circle of friends. It can be hard to see how it will all serve you later, but David Kobin made a discovery on the day of his graduation from Stuyvesant High School in New York City. "I was in my cap and gown, thinking only of all the rest and relaxation coming my way in the summer before college. The program began with the usual speeches about what an important day it was and how we were taking a huge step on the path to our futures. This went in one ear and out the other. All I cared about was getting into a cool restaurant for some lunch.

"But then came the awards ceremony. It seemed as though every student but me had done something great. There were National Merit Scholars, Westinghouse finalists, and every other prestigious recognition possible—but there were none for me, and it hurt. I suddenly felt that I had wasted four years of my life, years full of potential, with chance after chance to go beyond what was minimally required. I remembered all the ads for clubs to join, committees to be on, advanced classes to take, and I passed them all up. I used to think that only nerds joined those organizations, or that I didn't have time, or that I'd join the next one. But idle time passes rapidly, and before I knew it, it was senior year and I had never pushed myself. I lived a static life of TV and procrastination. With only one year of high school left and college applications sent out, there didn't seem to be any point to changing my lifestyle. So I didn't.

"At the close of the graduation ceremony, I was left with nothing but guilt and shame. I had failed myself and all those who ever had any faith in me. I decided then and there that college would be different. I am proud to say that so far I have stuck to the plan. When there's a conference or an ad for a club that interests me, I go; when I get an assignment, I put every bit of effort I can muster into it and more. TV and procrastination have become things of the past, and my free time is spent doing extra work and activities—there is no such thing as idle time. A year ago, I would have laughed at what I'm saying. That could never be me. But now it is me, and I am proud to say so. The funny thing is, I love every minute of it. Every assignment is a welcomed challenge, and every pressure a welcomed hurdle on my path to success. Sometimes I stumble, but every day brings me closer to the finish line."

Social Issues

High school is a whirlwind of experiences that have different effects on different people. Some people adjust to the new environment by throwing themselves into all kinds of activities. Some withdraw, keeping to themselves and focusing on what they are comfortable with—their studies or a certain subject or hobby. Many see high school as more of a social opportunity than anything else. Your high school experience probably has a stronger focus on friends and social activities than any of your previous schools, partly because you forge stronger bonds of friendship as you become more independent and begin to break away from the shelter of your family, and partly because the added component of biological change you are experiencing may draw you into relationships more complex than you have ever experienced before.

This strong focus on friends and groups can create both great fun and painful rejection. Dominic Ciresi, a college student at Northwestern University, found support and fun with his group of boarding school friends. "When I was in high school I had four really good friends, and we would get together in the dorm every night and drink a gallon of Kool-Aid. It got to be a kind of ritual for us—we never missed it. We would talk over what was going on, and what had happened that day." Angela Dorn, a corporate attorney, had some tougher times with the social scene at the Rosati-Kain School in St. Louis, Missouri. "I had a lot of fear socially, because I felt like a geek. To top it off, I moved to a different city in the middle of high school, which made it very difficult to meet people. It was pretty awful, actually. I didn't make friends right away because there were cliques already established. I hung out with other girls who felt like outsiders as well because their situations were similar to mine."

It can be intimidating when groups of students travel in packs and maintain allegiances only to one another, excluding you and others, and unfortunately it happens all the time, as Angela and Jim found out. Somehow everyone else's view of you seems to be the most important thing going. "I wish I had known not to be so concerned with what others thought of me and more concerned with what I think of myself," says Eileen Cook, an independent consultant on organizational health and workplace disability who went to high school in Traverse City, Michigan. "My entire high school life was spent mimicking what I thought others wanted from me, how they thought I should dress, speak, and so on. One student stands out in my mind when I think of that environment—his name was Dennis, and he had a learning disability. He wore the wrong things, he was shy, and he wasn't good-looking. He was the butt of jokes from the whole school. I never personally made fun of him, but I also couldn't be bothered to return his smiles or his attempts to reach out by saying hi.

"When I look back, I realize he was one of the most noble spirits I have ever known. He always offered to help—he cleaned up after the band and ran stage crew for the plays. He was nice to everyone, even the people who were nasty to him. He died in an accident, and everybody had one brief flash of guilt and then forgot him. Later I realized that it takes far more courage to be your own person and to be kind in a hostile world, as he did, than to follow the accepted path." Breaking away from the social bondage of high school involves being yourself no matter what other people think you should do—it's something not too many people can do, but it's worth trying.

"Something I really hate about high school is how certain people are not open to differences and creativity," says Melissa Rekas, a student at Centennial High School in Ellicott City, Maryland. "They think everyone should be the same, look the same, wear the same things, do the same things, or they're not worthy to talk to. My friends and I just try to ignore those kinds of people—I mean, we're nice to them, we try to be nice to everybody, but when they act like that we don't pay attention. I know that it's best to be myself. Also, rumors spread like crazy. People get half the story and make up the other half—everything gets blown up. You hear stories about yourself from people you don't even know, and they are hardly true!"

Responsibility

High school gives you a chance to take on more responsibilities on your way to having full responsibility for yourself as an adult. Responsibility comes with the knowledge you are building—the more you know, the more you can take charge, and the more often others will expect that you will.

Right now you are developing your sense of the world. You can already take care of most of your daily needs and activities. You are learning how to get around on your own, whether you drive or take buses or trains. You may know how to care for younger children. You can often do your homework without help. You draw on a huge amount of knowledge every day that you may not even think about.

You've come a long way from a few years ago! Think about the sixth grade. There wasn't much you could do on your own. The places you could go by yourself were limited. You probably didn't have a handle on tasks such as cooking or cleaning. You often needed help with your homework. You weren't able to be responsible for others younger than yourself. You didn't know too much about how to handle emergencies. You relied on adults for just about everything.

Now that your age and knowledge have brought you greater responsibility, you probably have all kinds of different reactions to it. Sometimes you want more of it. "Something that's hard about being in high school is that we're not kids anymore, but still our parents are on us about work and grades, and they don't let us do certain things," says Melissa. "We want freedom and respect." Sometimes responsibility can be a burden. But however you feel about it, responsibility is more than just an obligation. It is a golden opportunity to learn something new about yourself through how it makes you feel.

Deena Mottola, an intern at the Legal Assistance Foundation in Chicago with a degree in history, found herself occupied with an obligatory family responsibility. "When I was in high school, my mother had two babies and then went back to work. It became my responsibility to take care of the kids. They were really the most important thing in my life back then, even though I resented having that responsibility at that young an age. It was as if I had children of my own and was raising them. I felt responsible for making sure they had the proper upbringing, because I didn't think my parents were doing such a great job. Now I feel no great urgency to have a family because I feel like I already raised one when I was a teenager."

High school brings a variety of responsibilities. Some you want, like driving on your own or staying out later at night. Some can be more of a burden, like an increasingly difficult work load at school. I chose, and wanted, the responsibility of baby-sitting, but it sometimes led to a burden I didn't anticipate. One of the mothers who hired me to baby-sit was a great seamstress, and I took care of her kids in exchange for sewing lessons, which was a great incentive for me. I enjoyed being responsible for the kids and I wanted to learn to be responsible for making clothes for myself, because my mom said I could have all the clothes I wanted if I could make them.

The burden came because the older of the two kids, David, had autism—a mental disorder that put him into his own world where it was often hard to reach him. After his parents left, he used to run around shouting my name, throwing things, and scaring his little brother. Sometimes he would go to the bathroom on the floor and then run around laughing. It took all my patience to be calm with him, and he scared me. I could never predict what he would do. One day I took both boys to the park to play. I was feeling pretty miserable because I had just had my braces tightened and my mouth hurt like crazy. After we played on the swings, we went for a drink at the water fountain and out of nowhere David came up and hit me in the mouth—it hurt and I burst into tears. When his mom came home that afternoon, he shouted, "I hit Carol Carter and made her cry!" I started crying all over again in front of his mom.

Working with those two taught me a lot about how much strength and compassion it takes to be responsible. It was hard to deal with David, but I knew it was important, since he had so much to give even though he could not control his behavior. He needed more love and care than other children. When I became able to look at the situation through his eyes, I was sure that he saw a confusing world, and I understood how much he wanted people other than his parents to be able to relate to him. That is what I felt I was able to ultimately achieve with David. I'm glad I didn't quit and give in to my discouragement and fear.

Some responsibilities come from teachers or parents when they decide that you're ready, and sometimes your intuition tells you you are ready to take the step on your own. Either way, you make the choice to accept the responsibility and carry it out. Garth Kravits, an actor and singer in New York City, was given an important responsibility by one of his teachers at Magruder High School in Rockville, Maryland. "There weren't too many classes I was into in high school; the only thing that really made me happy was acting. My drama teacher asked me to teach a beginning acting class my senior year. He gave me the chance to take on responsibility for more than just myself, and I discovered that I really loved to teach other people what I knew and to inspire them to be creative."

Rebecca Lemberger, a student at Syracuse University, New York, earned the responsibility of being the editor in chief of her high school yearbook. "It was an immense honor. I had special privileges—an office, a permanent hall pass, and an excuse to get out of class. With all the excitement, I failed to realize that I had my work cut out for me! My assignment was to choose photographs and plan all 336 pages. I had to organize my time, distribute assignments, orchestrate events, and time everything perfectly so as not to miss a deadline. I learned how to deal with others, how to compromise and manage costs with my adviser, who limited my budget, how to be understanding and encouraging, and most of all, how to acknowledge my own faults. I was a leader to whom people looked for advice and approval. Sometimes this bothered me, and I wished I could have someone else make the difficult decisions. But in time I realized that the things I learned would stay with me for my entire life."

Talk about three responsibilities that you have taken on, or that have been given to you, since you started high school. How does each make you feel? Do you like them or dislike them? Would you like to change them, drop them, or expand them? Is change even an option? (If you are a member of a club, you may be able to resign easily; but you cannot get out of doing your schoolwork.)

Responsibility #1: _____

What do I feel? _____

_____

_____

_____

What have I learned about myself? _____

_____

_____

Responsibility #2: _____

What do I feel? _____

_____

_____

_____

What have I learned about myself? _____

_____

_____

Responsibility #3: _____

What do I feel? _____

_____

_____

_____

What have I learned about myself? _____

_____

_____

Fears

Every student, at one time or another, experiences fear as a part of living with high school—usually fear of failing or fear of what is going to happen in the future. For Cynthia Nordberg, now the associate director of an inner-city youth ministry in Chicago, fear of the future temporarily prevented her from moving ahead in her life. "Throughout high school I planned to attend college, but when graduation came, I couldn't do it. I had no idea why, but college seemed like a place for people much smarter than I was, and I was convinced I couldn't handle it. I had received good grades in school, had good friends, and a family that supported me, and still my fear of failing held me back from furthering my education." No matter what your background, you probably have some apprehension about where you are going.

Fear of the future can be about your future after high school or even in high school—what you are going to participate in this year, what classes you are going to take next year, if you are going to be accepted by the important group of friends this fall, or if your grades will improve. Fear of failing can affect your attitude toward classes, making an athletic team, asking someone out on a date, taking the PSATs or SATs or other tests, or achieving success in your extracurricular pursuits.

As scary as it is, fear of failure can be a positive force in your life—it can help you prepare adequately for the challenge. "The worst day of my life was the Monday after Thanksgiving when the varsity basketball team roster would be posted up at noon in the gym," says Dale Ellis, now a college student at Syracuse University in New York. "I was a returning member to the team, so I was not really worried, although I didn't work on my skills during the off-season because I chose to focus on work and football. I figured I would get into the weekend tryouts and then work my way into the starting lineup. No returning member ever gets cut the next year!

"After lunch, my friends and I went to the gym to look at the list. I looked up and down about ten times but could not find my name. My worst nightmare had come true. I talked to my coach, and he said that he did not think I improved enough to help this year's team. I thought he was full of it, and felt I could still beat half the team in my sleep, but in the next few painful weeks I learned a lot from this experience. It taught me never to take something for granted, no matter how sure I may be about the situation. I also learned that if you want something, you cannot take any vacations. You have to constantly work toward making it a reality. Any half-assed preparation just will not do."

Some people have to face fear on a more basic level. To Joseph Smith, a junior at Senne High School in Chicago, fear is a familiar emotion. "Once when I was coming out of my house, I saw a dude that looked about seventeen years old running down the sidewalk. Another guy was running after him and shot him four times. I walked over there because I wondered if he was someone I knew. He wasn't, but seeing him bleeding bothered me a lot. I was afraid to go out of my house for several days after that. I think he was shot because of drugs—drugs are everywhere here. On my block there's someone at every corner

selling them, out in the open daylight. I have no idea how they get away with it. Fast money lures kids into selling—you make minimum at McDonald's, but you can stand around all day selling drugs and make a couple hundred.

"There are gang fights at my school sometimes, and the security guards usually break them up. Commuting to school is the most tense part of my day. I travel an hour and a half on the el, and sometimes fights break out on the train. I feel nervous knowing that at any moment something can happen. I have done some bad things, like hang out with the wrong people late at night, but I never wanted to sell drugs because I was afraid I would be killed. God has given me the strength to stay away from things that pull me down. Sometimes when I want to do bad, something inside me tells me no, don't do it. I didn't use to hear that voice."

What Is the Point of High School?

A lot of students ask themselves, "What can I learn from taking this class?" "Why am I here?" "How can this do anything for me?" I wondered these things myself as a high school student. We all know the standard answers: It's important to be well educated, associate with others, join in activities, and take responsibility for our lives. Even if you've heard all that before, you may still feel that you are in high school because it's expected. I know that I felt I was in school because that's what I was supposed to do. I felt like just another sheep being herded along. I was there because I had to be.

Coping with the high school system requires a lot of ingenuity, but you can find your way through it all. Success doesn't mean having the perfect experience—no one does. Success involves capitalizing on the good opportunities, bypassing the dead spots, and turning around the problematic situations. Whoever started the rumor that the perfect high school experience exists was lying! Therefore, your challenge is to discover what you can value about high school and not to give up when you come up against roadblocks. As you read this book, you will learn about how to cope with problem situations such as a troublesome relationship with a teacher, a boring class, irritating groups of friends, or a subject you dislike. Society's system has put you in high school. Don't let yourself be dragged through—make the system serve *you*. Decide what high school means to you and make the most of it.

As you read, you will come upon information about how to take advantage of what high school can offer you, such as:

- Education
    - Learning how to get the most out of both exciting and boring classes
    - Dealing with teachers, administrators, counselors
    - Finding mentors
    - Cooperating with others
- Friends
    - Coping with cliques and social politics
    - Discovering how your friends help you know yourself
    - Experiencing peer pressure
    - Responding to diversity in your school and your world
    - Dating
- Yourself
    - Keeping in shape through sports and athletics
    - Joining clubs and groups that you like
    - Knowing who you are
    - Becoming more independent

If there is anything high school means to you that I haven't yet mentioned, write it here:

_____

_____

_____

_____

_____

_____

What Do You Have to Offer?

Actually, at the most basic level, the most important thing you have to offer your high school experience is your presence! Just being there is the first step to opening yourself up to what you can learn, even though it's not always easy or fun or exciting. Learning to keep at the things that don't come easily will take you a long way toward success. Sandra McCullough, a high school student in New York City, had to draw on some special resources to pull herself back in. "I left the high school I was in before. I just didn't feel like going at the time. I decided to go back because I was having a baby and I wanted to be able to help her to the fullest. I know there will be things that she won't know and I wanted to be able to tell her the answers to those things."

My point in writing this book is not to paint a rosy, cheery picture of high school and deny the validity of your negative feelings and experiences. I know that everything you feel, both good and bad, is true, because I have been there. As a teenager in high school, I wasted a lot of time and risked never finding my niche in life. I felt insecure and undirected. But through the help of my brother and others, I made it through and found myself and my confidence. I hope this book can provide similar encouragement for you.

Although we may or may not have much in common, we all share the experience of going to high school and being a teenager. That's pretty basic, but on that maybe we can build a mutual understanding to help us learn from one another's experiences. Reading this book will throw some challenges at you—and the biggest one is to realize your dreams. I want to psych you up for making the most of all the wonderful, talented, intense things you are. Your end of the bargain is to keep an open mind about the world and other people and to find a way to realize that you are important, valuable, and worthwhile.

·2·

GETTING ADJUSTED
Figuring Yourself Out

I have grown happier with every year of my life as though gradually conquering something in myself, for certainly my miseries were not made by others, but were a part of my own mind.
WILLIAM BUTLER YEATS
Poet
1865–1939

When William Butler Yeats was a young boy growing up in Sligo, Ireland, life was anything but happy. At school, Yeats was a poor student who never got his work done, and everybody knew it. To the shame and disbelief of his family and himself, he was unable to read until he was nine years old. On the playground, things were just as bad. His schoolmates considered him delicate, awkward, and just plain weak. He was rarely picked to participate in games and, because of his sickly appearance, fared just as badly when it came to girls. He almost always felt embarrassed. Over time, he became filled with anger and hurt; he was terribly shy and uncertain of himself. He withdrew.

At home, it was no better. His father, a painter, was a lifelong "starving artist" who had a strong opinion on almost every topic under the sun. Not only was he opinionated, he was also determined to have Willy accept his views on politics, religion, values, and other topics without question. When Willy resisted, his father would become angry and sometimes even violent with him.

Times were also bad financially. The family often had trouble trying to make ends meet, and the Yeatses eventually had to leave Willy's beloved Sligo for faraway London. In addition to being homesick, this native Irishman now had to suffer the taunts of being called a "foreigner" by his British peers. He didn't know quite who he was or where he belonged.

Some of you may be able to identify with William Butler Yeats. You may be coping with unfamiliar environments or family pressures commonly encountered during high school. If you're confused about yourself, you're not alone. How can you begin to find a path that makes sense to you? Yeats built on his self-knowledge—and eventually he turned almost every minus in his life to a plus.

As a student in London, Yeats soon realized that he was never going to be able to win athletic awards or top the popularity charts. He started to explore what he *could* do. What activities made him happy? Writing, mostly. If he had to spend time alone because he didn't have many friends, how could he fight the loneliness by filling the time with something that he enjoyed doing? He could explore his soul and record his thoughts in poetry.

In time, he developed a powerful poetic voice, and his accomplishments helped him build his confidence and his sense of himself. The trials of his youth fed into writings that his readers could relate to on a deeply personal level. Partly because of the prejudice he encountered, he developed a strong pride in his roots that immersed him in Irish nationalism and culture; Irish subjects later became one of the most characteristic and endearing features of his poetry. Although his youth was a painful time of adjustment, he emerged successfully because of his faith in himself. Not only was he able in later years to reconcile his relationship with his father, who became a friend, but, more important, he found happiness and meaning in his life. In a poem entitled "The Coming of Wisdom with Time," Yeats writes:

> Though leaves are many, the root is one;
> Through all the lying days of my youth
> I swayed my leaves and flowers in the sun;
> Now I may wither into the truth.

Discovering Yourself

From Yeats, whom the world knows today as Ireland's greatest poet, you can learn about adjusting to life's pressures through looking within yourself for the truth about who you are. One of the things that you can draw from high school is the time and opportunity to develop *self-knowledge*. As you grow older, life becomes more complicated and challenging, and knowing yourself allows you to have some control over *how* difficult it becomes. You may not have thought that having an opportunity to look within yourself was part of the high school experience, but you learn about yourself in high school through the *environment* in which you live and work, *what you do,* and *how you relate to others.* You build self-knowledge without even thinking about it.

Your Environment

The "you" that you know today has evolved from a number of sources. Some aspects of your personality are yours from birth. Others you develop as a result of the environment in which you live. Your environment both illuminates and shapes who you are. As you react to things and events in your environment, you discover what you do and do not like. Where you grow up—your home, your neighborhood, your school, where you spend your free time—becomes a part of you and affects how you think and act.

For example, as Angela Dorn found out, the type of school you attend may give you opportunities that can change you. Her family moved from Chicago to St. Louis just before her junior year of high school, and she chose to attend an all-girls school, which was a real switch from her previous coed high school. "I noticed the difference right away, and thought it was great. The girls were in charge of everything. I wasn't worried about having to outdo some guy all the time. I ended up being the vice president of our Senior Council—and I'm not sure I would have done that at a coed school. It was better for me because I didn't date a lot in high school, and not having boys around relieved the dating pressure somewhat. All in all, it really helped me focus on academics."

Your home environment has a strong effect on you as well. Having lots of time to herself as a child has helped to create Becky Amato's need for personal time as an adult. "I was raised an only child, and I really enjoy the little bit of time I can find to be on my own. It is the only time I feel truly at ease." Becky attended Chicago's Oak Park River Forest High School and is now studying radio, TV, and film at Northwestern University.

Think about your own environment. What do you like best about it? What turns you off? What do your answers to those questions tell you about yourself? For each place in your life, give an example of something it has taught you about yourself or how it has shaped who you are.

Home: _____

_____

_____

_____

School: _____

_____

_____

_____

Work or Recreation: _____

_____

_____

_____

What You Do

Activities at school or during free time, your jobs or your homework, events with family or friends—all of these situations teach you something about who you are. As your experiences pile up, so does your knowledge about yourself.

Heather Pollack learned something about herself during her years at Bloomington High School South, Indiana, that shaped the career she has today as a free-lance set dresser for film and television. "I started working when I was very young—but if I didn't like a job, I didn't stay. I worked several jobs before I finally found my dream job through a friend. I worked selling popcorn at a movie theater, and it changed my life in so many ways. I had always loved movies—and I realized that there was a way you could make money in film, even if it was simply by managing a movie theater. Also, I learned that there were other people who shared my interest in movies."

Gwenan Wilbur, a graduate of Walter Johnson High School in Bethesda, Maryland, learned a great deal about herself from her dance classes. "I was a very serious student of ballet. It taught me discipline, and my body was in incredible shape. In many ways it made me hyper-aware of my body. In some ways it made me more comfortable with myself because I was strong, and in shape, but on the other hand, I was always painfully aware of my physical inadequacies for dancing. There are certain very strict requirements for your body if you want to be a professional dancer, and my hips were always too square, and my arms too short. Because of this, I realized when I was about fifteen that I could never make this a career. Even so, I continued training very seriously, because by then it was a way of life."

You will also make discoveries about yourself from doing things that you don't necessarily choose or even want to do: a chore your parents give you, a school assignment, or a family trip. If you don't like what you're doing, what specifically turns you off? If you discover that an activity seems to suit you, how else can you work that activity into your life? What kinds of things inspire dread in you, and what makes you want to do more?

Learn from your activities. Whether you play on the basketball team, have to take a math class every year, read books beyond those your teachers assign in school, take care of your baby brother, or shop with your friends, you can find clues to yourself everywhere. Pick one thing that you really love to do, and one thing that you have to do. What valuable information have you discovered about yourself from those two activities?

I like to _____

This activity has taught me _____

_____

_____

I have to _____

This activity has taught me _____

_____

_____

How You Relate to Others

Your friends, teachers, or relatives can also teach you about yourself. Your friendships are especially revealing, because though you don't choose relatives or teachers for the most part, you do choose your friends. You might not even be aware of actually making choices— often it seems as if friendships just happen by chance. Figuring out who you like to be around, and who likes to be around you, is part of discovering your individuality.

What kind of people are your best friends? What do you like most about them? What do you admire? What draws you to them? Sometimes you admire traits in your friends that are similar to yours, and sometimes you are drawn toward people with traits that you don't have but would like to. Sarah Lyman Kravits says, "I realized at some point during high school that I had a lot of assertive people as friends. Since I have always had a problem sticking up for myself, I figured that I chose those friends partially so that I could learn something from their strength and straightforward style."

What quality do you seek in friends that you share? _____

_____

What quality do you seek that you don't share? _____

_____

How do your friends see you? What do they like about you? What do you do that annoys them? You can learn a lot from their observations and opinions, even if you don't always agree with them. Has a friend ever said something about you that surprised you but that you came to believe was true? What was it?

_____

_____

Relationships give you the chance to learn how to cooperate, compromise, and work as a member of a team. No school or career field excludes all human contact. If you know what degree of interaction makes you comfortable, you are one step further along. "My freshman year, I was on the women's track team," says Angela Dorn, "and this team gave me a feeling of 'working together' with other people. Looking back, I think that sports are one of the best things a person can do in high school."

Romantic relationships can teach you about yourself, as Cherry Hill, New Jersey, native Dustin Grimm found out. "The most positive aspect of my high school experience was my relationship with my senior-year girlfriend, Kelly. It taught me how to be understanding, how to communicate, and how to express my emotions. It taught me about myself—I now know that I am a deeply emotional individual and that I don't dwell on superficial qualities. I learned that I was capable of dealing with someone on an adult level—working out our schedules so that we could get things done and still spend time together was one of the most difficult things about our relationship."

Cliff Balanag learned a lot from working with a group for a class project at his Stockton, California, high school. "Two weeks before my high school graduation, my calculus teacher divided us into groups and assigned presentations. My group had the class valedictorian, two of my friends, and myself. I thought we were going to be a great group because we all knew one another's habits. At first we were focused and set goals for ourselves. But as we progressed, my friends and I became intimidated by the valedictorian. She wasn't overpowering or rude, but she didn't seem to care much for the group—she just cared about her grade. When we met, she would go on to the next problem while the rest of us tried to solve the previous one. She ended up contributing the most while we just listened. We did things her way.

"This made me realize that when it comes to group work, I get intimidated by someone who takes charge. I don't know the reason for this. I had ideas to share, but I never spoke up, and just did things the way Lily wanted them done. I was more of a follower than a contributor. I no longer keep quiet when working with other people within a group. I try to be more outspoken with my ideas. I try not to feel intimidated by someone taking charge, and try just to take advantage of what I can learn from them."

You can learn a lot as you work with others toward a common goal, whether it's a class project, an athletic event, or a family chore. Do you like working cooperatively with a group, or does having to depend on others annoy you? Do you respond well to pressure, or do you get nervous and make mistakes? Is all your confidence based on winning, or are you happy just playing? Chances are your feelings may be mixed, depending on the activity and who has joined you in it.

How does working with a group make you feel?

_____

_____

Interests and Talents

Taking an honest, specific look at what you like to do and what you are good at doing is another important step in discovering who you are. It's not always easy—many people don't bother to do it carefully enough and spend much of their lives doing things that don't really interest them. The earlier you figure out a few things that turn you on, the more likely you will be to choose a career and lifestyle that make sense for who you are, to make a living at what you love to do, and to be a generally happy and satisfied person.

INTEREST, noun.
  a feeling of being drawn to something; liking or being curious about something
TALENT, noun.
  an apparently natural power or gift in the learning or doing of anything

---

It has been said that nothing great in life is ever achieved without enthusiasm. Your job is to figure out what you truly feel enthusiastic about—or might feel enthusiastic about if you had the chance. What you like to do and what you do well are often closely linked—*you usually do the best at what you like to do.* James Morris, a junior at Whitney Young High School in Chicago, knows—and likes to do—what he does well. "The things I enjoy most in school are English and drama. I really enjoy writing, and in my spare time I write for fun. I think I might like to be a writer someday. Also, one of my greatest skills is my ability to talk to people. There was a fight at our school between two girls, and at some point their boyfriends became involved and pulled out guns. The fight was escalating rapidly, and I jumped in the middle and talked them out of using their weapons. I'm diplomatic and know how to talk, and it helps me get respect at school and in the neighborhood."

Take Your Time

You don't have to decide right this second what you want to do for the rest of your life. Just begin to consider your interests and talents in broad, expansive terms. Eventually, you will need to consider other factors when choosing a career. Where do you want to live? With what kind of people do you enjoy working? How much income will satisfy your needs? The more you know yourself, the more easily the answers will come to you. Elissa Barnes, a student from Woodmere, New York, happened upon a talent while looking for an elective. "My guidance counselor said I was one credit short. I told her to put me in an art, but she said none of those classes were open, and the closest one to it was advertising. I decided to try the course out, but at first I felt weird, because I didn't know anyone in the class.

"After a few weeks, I really started liking it. We made posters for upcoming school events. I found that when I used my artistic talent and humor, I got a lot of responses. Then I got a taste of marketing when the business department decided to make a Disneyland Food Court, and we had to create a booth—we decided to do 'Minnie's Diet Delight,' with all diet foods. The second the fair started, we were packed. We did not have a minute to sit down. Since that day, I have wanted to become involved with advertising and marketing. The whole project—the advertising, research, investment, and joy of profit—truly excited me."

Many different experiences can spark your imagination and help you figure out your interests. I learned something about myself from an experience as a camp counselor.

On our first night of camp, we sat around a campfire singing songs. It was the first time many of these kids had been away from home, and they were realizing what it meant to be away from and to truly miss their friends and family. Later that night, the campers in my group and I sat in a circle on the floor and talked about how each person felt. One girl, Leslie, was very quiet and didn't share her thoughts with everyone else. She and I went elsewhere to talk after the rest of the campers had gone to bed. Starting to cry, she told me that her parents were going through a divorce. It made her feel very neglected and sad to see two people she loved in the middle of such conflict. She and I spent a lot of time together the rest of the week. After camp was over, we wrote to each other every couple of weeks.

This was the first time I realized how much I enjoyed counseling and listening to people. I knew I helped to soothe Leslie's pain that week.

I also understood the role I played with the growing pains the other campers were experiencing. At the end of our week together, there were a lot of tears—many of them from me—because we didn't want this time to end. We had all grown and learned from one another. Now, almost twenty years later, I know that this experience was my first clue to one of my most basic interests: working with people younger than myself to help them make sense of themselves and their world.

Take Your Own Personal Inventory

Here are some specific questions that can help you define what you like and what you do well. As you answer them, you will build your own unique and personal inventory of interests and talents.

INVENTORY, noun.
  1. an appraisal, as of one's skills or personal characteristics
  2. a listing of what one has in stock

These were my primary interests in high school:

1. Talking on the phone
2. Going out with my friends
3. Going shopping

These interests may seem less than honorable, but they're honest. And later in life, in college and my career, I worked primarily with people —on the phone and in person. Shopping I grew to hate as an adult. So you see, some things change! Give yourself credit for what you like to do and keep exploring. It doesn't matter if your talents and interests change. What matters is that you are confident in yourself at every stage of growth.

My Likes and Dislikes

1. What I most like about people is _____

_____

_____

Favorite person? Why? _____

_____

_____

2. What I most dislike about people, ranked first to last, is _____

_____

_____

Least-favorite person? Why? _____

_____

_____

3. What I like most about school and/or working is _____

_____

_____

4. What I most dislike about school and/or working is _____

_____

_____

5. My favorite activities are _____

_____

_____

6. My least-favorite activities are _____

_____

_____

What Interests Me

1. I am curious about _____

    _____

    _____

2. I spend time thinking about _____

    _____

    _____

3. I am concerned about _____

    _____

    _____

4. I am fascinated by _____

    _____

    _____

5. I like to read/write about _____

    _____

    _____

My Talents and Skills (at school, at home—anywhere)

1. I feel most confident about myself when I am _____

    _____

    _____

2. I'm usually considered among the leaders when I'm _____

_____

_____

3. People compliment me when I _____

_____

_____

4. The things I get encouraged to do most often are _____

_____

_____

5. My best skills, ranked first to last, are _____

_____

_____

6. The skills I don't have and want most to acquire, ranked first to

last, are _____

_____

_____

It's not necessary at this point to draw any conclusions. The important thing is that you've begun the identification process. With so much living ahead of you, there is plenty of time and opportunity to match your interests and talents to potential careers.

If you would like to find out what your responses to the personal inventory indicate when you look at them all together, use the following system. Put a "P" next to each response that in any way deals with people. For example, place a "P" next to a response that identifies "helping others" as a skill or interest. Next, put an "I" next to any response that deals with ideas or information. If you listed as a skill "helping others find books in the library" as a skill or interest, place both a "P" and an "I" next to this response. Finally, put an "O" next to a response identifying your interest in objects, such as "working on cars" or "computer software." If one of your responses is "helping others install computer software," put both a "P" and an "O" next to this response.

Next, examine each of your "P" responses as a group, each of your "I" responses as a group, and each of your "O" responses as a group. Does any pattern emerge? Clusters of responses may indicate a particular interest or dislike, a certain talent or area of limited ability. If you have no responses listed under the "People" category, for example, a career as a sales agent may not be your calling (let's hope you haven't already ordered your business cards!).

Keep Learning about Yourself

Every human being is in a constant state of change. Your interests shift, your talents grow and expand, your dislikes fade. Here are some strategies that will keep you aware of yourself:

1. Really Talk—with Friends and Others

You won't have the time or the desire to talk about the "meaning of life" with everyone you meet. But sometimes it makes sense for you to talk—really talk—to a friend, a family member, a teacher, or anyone else about what's on your mind. It doesn't have to be about a problem. It might be about an insight you've had, or something you've enjoyed doing or seeing. Go ahead and share what you are thinking. When you express your thoughts, you clarify them for yourself. Plus, it might invite a response from which you can learn something.

2. Write Down Your Thoughts

When you record your thoughts on paper, you can chart and analyze your plans, deeds, fears, and dreams. Write all about yourself in a journal, and then reread what you have written a month or more from now. You'll be surprised at what you learn about yourself! Write about your expectations and aspirations, your disappointments and fears. Write about the world as you see it. Be blunt and honest.

If a daily or weekly journal isn't your thing, you might consider taking up the lost art of letter writing. Perhaps you have a love interest in a different city, or a relative you want to stay in touch with. Perhaps there is a pen-pal system you can hook up with. Whoever your readers may be, committing your thoughts to paper challenges you to confront yourself.

3. Analyze Your Experiences in Personal Terms

The next time you see a movie or hear a track of your favorite new CD, think about how you feel about it and why. Compare the words, or the story line, with your own beliefs and experiences. Do you agree with what is said or depicted or not? Do you have a different idea about life? In the world of artistic creation or in day-to-day life, you will be constantly encountering different viewpoints. Let those different viewpoints focus your attention inward. Everything that you observe can help you affirm or modify your own beliefs.

4. Seek Out Time Alone

By taking even a little time off every day to think things through for yourself, you can become more aware of yourself and the world around you. Spending time alone on a regular, daily basis—even if it's just fifteen minutes—may help you clear your head and come up with solutions to problems that would just grow larger if you ignored them. Do whatever relaxes you in your alone time. "When I'm by myself, I write, read, sleep, and generally relax," says Becky Amato.

5. Consider Different Perspectives

Keep your mind open. When someone else has a different idea about something, try to see the situation from that person's perspective. Challenge the status quo. Challenge yourself. Maybe your ideas will become stronger because of the challenge, or maybe they will change and develop for the better. Don't assume that your ideas or perspectives are correct without challenge.

Finding Confidence

When I surveyed high school students about what bothered them most in high school, they cited feeling insecure about themselves as one of their primary worries. Even the seemingly cool and confident athletes and "popular" people had concerns about being accepted and fitting in. Sometimes people mistake cockiness for confidence. Don't believe it. Everyone has doubts about themselves.

CONFIDENCE, noun.
  1. belief in one's own abilities
  2. reliance on one's own powers

The first step in finding, and building, your confidence is recognizing that *you are special.* You have something unique to offer to yourself and to the world. Many people, as they move through childhood, hear this message from their parents and families. Parents and others tell us that our thoughts and accomplishments are useful. When we fail, they assure us that failure is a normal part of the process of learning, and that we are no less capable of achievement in the future. They accept and support us for who we are.

But not everyone has that kind of family support. If you don't, realizing that you are special, important, and unique might be harder for you to do. You will need to track down other sources of encouragement. Floris Suarez, a student at Manhattan Comprehensive Night High School in New York City, finds support in a close friend. "Maribell helps me sort things in many ways. For example, my father and I don't speak that much—we don't have much to say. When he drinks, he gets on my case and starts saying things that are not true. Maribell's advice is to speak up. She tells me if I don't tell my father how I feel, I won't be a happy person. When I have a problem or I'm stressed out by my boyfriend or parents, I ask her for advice."

Now, if someone had tried to convince me as a high school student that I was special and had a lot to offer, I would never have believed it. I would have described how attractive or funny or athletic or intelligent my other friends were, but I had a hard time identifying one or more of these things within myself. I spent a good deal of time thinking about what everybody *else* had and what I lacked in comparison, and it kept me from achieving as much as I could have.

In high school, I tried out for the gymnastics team. Even though I had taken gymnastics at the Y in junior high, this was a whole new competitive ball game. I didn't make the team, and at the tryout I decided that I was grossly unprepared compared with some of the others. The main problem was my lack of confidence. Although I had the desire and the drive to do well, I didn't believe in myself enough to take the physical risks that would raise my skills to a competitive level. I never quite made the most of my abilities. A few years later, I took up running, which required the drive that I already knew I had. Slowly, I developed the confidence in my stamina that eventually allowed me to finish the New York Marathon. Focusing on positive thoughts carried me through all 26.2 miles.

Almost all high school students fixate on everyone else's success rather than on their own value and achievements. It's a big roadblock. If you fall victim to this kind of lack of confidence, do yourself a favor and get over it. It's a no-win attitude that will prevent you from recognizing the talents you *do* have by focusing all of your energy on what you *don't* have. No matter how different you or I may be from the next person, we each have our own abilities, our own distinguishing features.

Experience itself can be one of the best confidence builders. Whenever you're disappointed by an outcome, just maintain a positive attitude, log the information, and keep going.

Miroslav Vucetic, a native of Split, Croatia, and a college student in New York State, used the drive he developed as a young swimmer to tackle an unexpected setback. "At the age of seven my mother took me to the swimming pool. Soon I became quite devoted, and began to practice seriously. At twelve I received a call to join Croatia's Junior National Team, and in the winter of 1990, when the manager of my swim club decided that we would go for a Christmas training trip in the mountains, I was so happy and looked forward to drastic improvement. But then I broke my leg skiing and all my dreams about having a successful swimming career suddenly fell apart. The doctors said I would have to stay away from the pool for six months.

"I thought it was the end of swimming for me, but some voice inside me said, 'Don't give up. You can do anything you want to.' So after two months I jumped into the pool still with my cast on and started to practice with great drive and effort. I had to handle school obligations and swimming practices as I worked to improve. To the joy of my teachers, parents, and coach, my persistence was rewarded that summer when I set three new Junior National records."

Your moments alone give you another opportunity to find and build confidence. Think about how you support the people you care about —you help them up when they're down, you tell them they can do whatever they set their minds to, you cheer them on in their dreams and goals. Now do the same for yourself. You deserve it just as much as your friends do! Take time to tell yourself how important you are and how talented you are. Pat yourself on the back for your successes, and console yourself for your failures. Tell yourself you'll do better the next time, and emphasize that you have a lot to give if you use your confidence to stay open to new experiences and new ways of doing things. You can be your own best cheerleader.

Give It Time

Learning to recognize the positive, unique strengths within you takes some time and some searching. They may not be so obvious to you right away. People spend their whole lives trying to build their confidence and figure out what makes them special. Some never succeed. The earlier you start, the better chance you have of getting to that place where your confidence allows you to try anything you want to do.

You'll have times when you don't believe in yourself. There will be people who bring you down and criticize you. You'll sometimes have trouble finding support and inspiration from others as well as inside. Just hang in there.

People have all different ways of working to keep up their faith in themselves. Some write in their diaries or talk to close friends. Sharifah Sams, a New York City high school student, turns to her religious life for help. "The most important person in my life is God. He helps me through my times of need and sadness—I talk to him every night. He helps me to believe in myself at so many times—when men bring me down, when I fear not being accepted and I change myself to fit in because of that fear, or the time when I failed school and was devastated and disappointed with myself."

Other students turn to clubs and groups that they like for reinforcement. "I was quiet and lacking in self-esteem before joining the East Ramapo Marching Band," says Mitch Polack, a recent high school graduate from Spring Valley, New York. "Our band director, Mike Smith, placed a strong emphasis on respect and commitment, and was a best friend any time you needed guidance. We learned that to get respect from the crowd, we had to respect ourselves first. I started as the assistant section leader of the lower brass, and by mid-season I had been promoted to secretary/treasurer. I have grown, and what I learned about respect and commitment will help me continue to believe in myself and grow some more."

Knowing yourself and having confidence in your value and your abilities will bring you happiness and success, because the best life for you lies down the path paved by your own talents and abilities, strengths and weaknesses, and likes and dislikes. The more you *find* yourself, the more you will have the ability to *be* yourself.

· 3 ·

REACHING OUT
Your Relationships with Others

[At school], more than actual study, my contact with girls my own age and the making of a few close friends were the most valuable part to me. . . . As I look back, I realize how awkward I was in making new contacts—not especially from shyness or any inhibitions on my part—but mostly from sheer ignorance and lack of experience in meeting adolescents.   DOROTHY REED MENDENHALL
                                                          Physician
                                                          1874–1964

When she entered Smith College as a freshman in 1891, Dorothy Reed Mendenhall had her first opportunity to make friends and to socialize with her peers. Never before had she had the chance to spend time with other students—she spent her high school years learning her lessons at home alone. Never before had she had any experience in making a friend her own age—she didn't know where to start, what to do, or how to fit in. She must have felt incredibly awkward when she encountered her first classmate at Smith. You may have experienced similar awkwardness when you entered a new high school, although you probably had at least a few chances to learn how to make friends in your younger years!

Before she attended college, Dr. Mendenhall's schooling had been anything but conventional. First of all, she received no formal education before her thirteenth birthday. Because of her father's illness and death and her own childhood sicknesses, she spent her early years at home, learning from exploration of the outdoors, helping with housework, caring for family members, and making handicrafts with her sister and governess. Her parents concentrated on her physical development and relied on her exposure to life's practical lessons. By the time she was thirteen, she knew how to read, write, and draw, but had no clue about

43

formal subjects such as mathematics and grammar. At that time, her parents decided to bring in a tutor to further her education. The tutor used the outdoors near the Reed house as her classroom, and for the next few years she was taught increasingly advanced levels of Latin, math, and English. This was Dorothy's "high school experience," and it provided her with an excellent education because her tutor was able to capture her interest and inspire in her a love of knowledge. Also, the tutor's emphasis on reading the classics in poetry and prose ended up providing her student with much more than what was required for entrance to Smith.

But there was something missing. There had been no one to hang out with. No one to study with. No one to compare notes with about the events that made her angry or confused, the successes that she worked so hard to achieve, and the mistakes that left her upset but more knowledgeable than before. People her own age played no part in her education.

Many people take for granted what a valuable resource friends can be—how friends can provide support, share their knowledge, and help solve problems. Other people want desperately to make friends, but are scared or unsure of how to go about it. But consider Dr. Mendenhall's example. Before college, she didn't really know what she was missing. When she got the chance to be around other students her own age, she realized how important friendships can be. While she didn't know much about making friends, her desire to do so helped her rise to the challenge. She gained a deep respect for her new friends.

Dorothy Reed Mendenhall began to experience the fullness of life when she started to share it with other people. Although she was mature intellectually and relatively self-aware before college, she was able to extend her self-knowledge through becoming friends with her classmates. Not surprisingly, Dr. Mendenhall chose a profession that involves interacting with and helping others. Even with all the other material she learned at Smith, she felt that the most important skill she had gained from her college experience was how to interact successfully with others. She did research at Johns Hopkins Medical School, and later she became a specialist in maternal and child health.

Relating to the People in Your Life

Almost everything you experience at school, at play, or at home involves relating to other people on some level. As you move through high school into college or a career and beyond, you will continue to encounter people on all levels of intimacy—from the people you pass on the street to the people you see every day hard at work to those with whom you choose to share your home. The more you know about yourself and how you relate to others, the more successful you will be in your relationships, both personal and professional.

Friends

When I was in high school, my friends and I hung out in a very tightly knit pack. When we weren't physically together, we were incessantly on the telephone. We were a family, connected by common experiences and shared interests. Our favorite way of getting around was my friend Leslie's old LTD, which could fit seven people comfortably. Leslie was the first to get her driver's license, so she became the designated chauffeur. We cruised around Tucson, Arizona, in this car, going on shopping mall pilgrimages, to football games at opposing teams' high schools, and to dessert parties and pig-outs at fast-food restaurants. We put one another first, above everything else, and we shared almost everything that happened as well as how we felt about it all.

Through their support for one another, friends often become a sort of family. "We are a special group because when one of us is in trouble everyone tries to help make the problem better," says Tamika Leslie, a New York City high school junior. "There are six of us. We all get together and chill out and eat and talk. Two of us have graduated and one of us dropped out to have a baby. The ones who are still in school go to classes together and chill in the bathroom." When you spend that much time with people, you develop strong ties.

"When I first started high school, I did not know too many people, and I thought that meeting new people would be hard," says Frank Caporrino, a college student at Syracuse in New York State. "But the people I met soon became my closest friends, because we did work together, played on teams together, and spent time on weekends just hanging out. I looked forward to going to school each day just to see these people and try to become better friends. We were always there to help each other out with school, girls, or anything else the average high school kid has problems with. We have all gone our separate ways, but the bonds we created in high school are stronger than ever. We keep in close touch, have advice for each other, and share stories about our different college experiences. Knowing that my friends will always be there no matter what happens helps me to get through each and every day."

You can learn from your friends. What you know and what your friends know, how you live and how they live can be very different. Maybe your parents are divorced and your best friend's parents have been married for twenty years, and you learn from each other what each kind of situation involves. Maybe you live in the suburbs and you learn about city living when you visit your friend's apartment there.

In high school, as in life, people tend to form groups or "cliques" based on common interests; the band people spend time with one another, the athletes and cheerleaders hang out together, the studious people do things with one another, and the not-so-studious people stick together, too. This is a generalization, of course—many people develop friendships with people from different groups. But cliques are always there, all different kinds, usually formed around similar interests, activities, physical appearances, lifestyles, or backgrounds.

The social groups with which you get involved can be a source of some of the most important lessons you will learn in your high school years. They can give you support, help, a good time, and a sense of belonging. Friends in a group can be loyal and supportive throughout your high school years, helping you to build your self-esteem and push yourself to achieve things that you might not otherwise have tried. You can learn about the hierarchy of power that forms in groups (who leads, who follows), a pattern that will continue to show up in your adult life, as well as about cooperation, compromise, and the commitment of friendship itself.

"I was part of the fun nerdy people," says Deena Mottola. "Our group was the only coed clique, and what was unique about it was that the boys and girls in our group hung out together because we really liked each other—not because we were sleeping together. This was very unusual in my high school, where typically girls hung out with girls and boys hung out with boys. Our group helped me get to know and care for friends of both sexes."

On the flip side, dealing with how students flock together and cling to one another can be a drag. It's pretty common for students to base their self-esteem on what others think—if they are accepted by a popular group, they feel important and proud, and if they are rejected, they feel unworthy. Certain groups can be pretty cruel about leaving out people that they don't think will fit, and that rejection can create misery. Even if you aren't obviously rejected, you may not feel comfortable in any of the popular groups, and the way that high school life focuses on group activities may cause you to be left out. Some people fight that trend by focusing on more private friendships with only a few selected people.

Gwenan Wilbur didn't quite fit into any of the groups at her school. "My serious study of ballet left me very socially isolated. The fact that my family moved every two years didn't help either. When I arrived at a new place, my pattern of social survival was to look around for a very non-threatening, supportive person and cling to her. That is how I found my best friend, and her very small group of friends. We ate lunch together and talked about the meaning of life. We did help and support each other, because it was not cool for girls to be unsociable."

What can make other people reject you? In high school, just about anything. Often it is something superficial, like your hair or clothing style, or what kinds of activities you like. Other times, groups will reject those who they think are too nerdy and studious or, if the group consists of brainy people, those who don't take their work seriously. And many times you just will have no idea why you didn't make it with a certain friend or group of friends, because people often won't bother to explain it to you.

Even though Lee Pomeroy had a hard time socially, she turned rejection into a plus later on. "I was not a part of any clique or social group in high school, and this was one of the most painful things about those years for me. But one piece of advice I would give to high school students is that just because you aren't popular today doesn't mean you won't have a fulfilling social life in the future. Even though I was painfully shy in high school, I kept busy outside school with activities like traveling with the Explorer Scouts and editing their newsletter, being an exchange student in Sweden, and reading a lot. I now have the most dynamic and exciting group of friends I could hope for—and they are all over the world. I value these friends very much because they are people I can count on and I love to be with."

When I was in high school, I loved having a lot of friends. But there were two groups with whom I didn't fit in very well—namely, the athletes and the students who cut class to smoke cigarettes in the parking lot. I wasn't an athlete and I didn't smoke, but over time, I became friends with people in both these circles, through other connections. Later on, when I went to my ten-year high school reunion, I was happy to see that time had erased even more of the lines of distinction between the stereotypical "jocks," "nerds," "freaks," and everyone else.

I found out at the reunion that, interestingly enough, high school had turned out to be the high point of life for some of the popular people, and they had had a hard time since graduating because they failed to identify new goals for themselves. On the other hand, one of the biggest troublemakers—a very smart goof-off who never applied himself in high school—went on to graduate from college, earn an M.B.A., and work for a major financial firm in San Francisco. One depressing surprise was that a very popular athlete, a year after graduation, had committed rape and robbery. He was still in prison. For the rest of us, it was a relief not to feel the pressures we felt in high school and to know that we pretty much accepted one another for who we were—full-time parents, professional people, welders, engineers, dental hygienists, flight agents, and members of many other varied professions. From our perspective ten years after, we realized that the four years of high school were only a short segment of our lives, and that we had plenty of time after that to make changes and learn how to understand ourselves.

One important thing to note about groups is that they don't always have your best interests at heart. From time to time, students find themselves doing something that doesn't feel right in order to become accepted (or stay accepted!) by a group. Even worse, the disagreeable "requirement" can be harmful and dangerous if it involves alcohol or drug use, reckless driving, sleeping around, cutting classes, or any illegal behavior. Just as harmful (to the mental health of everyone involved) is any teasing or verbal abuse of people belonging to different ethnic groups or economic classes, people who have special physical or mental challenges, or anyone who just doesn't seem to "fit in."

How can you avoid getting dragged into being someone you're not? It's not easy. One way of protecting yourself is to really look at the standards and the reputation of any particular group before you "sign up." You may want to be as popular or as cool as the group members, but consider these questions:

- Do you want to act as they do?
- Do you want to live by the same values and ethics that they do?
- Do you want other people to think of you as they think of them (however that may be)?

Take your time. If you decide you aren't comfortable with a group you've begun to hang around with, it's better to move on and make some new friends. That's easier said than done, but it's worth it in the long run, even if those you reject don't take kindly to rejection. People who like you only if you fit in with their behavior, attitude, or style of clothing probably don't care enough about the real you to be worth your time and energy.

For now, take a good look at who you are. If you are happy being a part of a group and have one that supports you, make the most of it. If you prefer to socialize on a smaller scale, locate two or three people with whom you can be yourself and feel accepted. Whoever you are, there are people out there who will relate to and accept the real you. Finding them through trial and error is part of the normal ups and downs of friendship. The more you know about yourself, the more you'll choose friends who stick by you and help you grow.

After some soul-searching and friend-searching, Angela Dorn found the circle of friends that made the most sense for who she really was: "I felt like I was a bit of a geek. I hung out with the debate team, which people considered the intellectual geeky set. The team was very important to me because it was the first time in my life that I felt really comfortable in a social group. They were all very academically motivated and competitive—and I think they encouraged me to be that way." There is a place for everyone, even though it usually takes a trip down a long and sometimes troublesome road to find.

Sunnyside High School student Shirley Saylor, who lives in Tucson, sums up what friendship means to her: "Being a friend is not as easy as you think. A friend, in my opinion, is someone who's there for you, who you can trust, someone who understands you, listens to you, cares about you, helps you, and never does anything to hurt you."

Family

"Family" means different things to different people. Some of you may be very close to your families and may live full-time with both parents and maybe a couple of siblings. Often, though, "family" will take on a less traditional meaning. Some high school students live with one parent, with or without a stepparent. Some live with aunts and uncles or grandparents. Some look toward an older sibling for support and guidance. And some have adoptive families or foster families. These days, the family may not be stable, either; you may have lived with several different versions of family in your lifetime. With so much change going on in your head and body, you need to find stability in your family, and it isn't always there.

It may be hard to focus on your family, or to remember that your family relationships are just as important as your friendships. You might tend to take your family members for granted—after all, they have been around for a long time, and you might often find them annoying or oppressive or controlling or nosy. But they are a part of your life no matter what.

Many of the people I spoke to felt alienated from their families, for different reasons. As I have mentioned, when I was in high school I resented my four older brothers' successes and for a long time didn't feel secure about turning to them for help or advice. One New York City student, Nelson Cruz, recently experienced the death of his mother and is having to cope with making it on his own. "The way I dealt with it was that I knew, as of then, I had become a man. I had to take care of myself because I feel the only person who was supposed to be there for me and provide for me was gone."

Others simply didn't feel understood by their parents, or they felt that the way their parents lived wasn't what they wanted. "My mother was the dominant force in our family, and she was an unhappy person," says Gwenan Wilbur. "Unhappiness and fighting were the norm in our household. My mother didn't have a career outside the home and didn't really love what she did [parenting]. Later, after being around strong female teachers who loved their jobs and their lives, I could see that unhappiness was not the norm, and I didn't have to be that way."

On the other hand, many people find strength in their family ties, no matter what kind of family they belong to. Even if you feel put off by your family members right now, you might not want to shut them out altogether. Give yourself time to get to know them as people. Although you may feel that they don't understand what you are going through, you might discover as you grow that they can offer you much-needed support and love. Manhattan Comprehensive Night High School student Kirk Jennings says, "My parents are my mentors because they support me. They tell me to finish what I start, and I'm graduating in June."

"My mother helps me every way she can," says Patrice Richards, a classmate of Kirk's. "She tells me everything she knows, and she gives me good advice in many things. I hope my mother is my good friend always." Amanda Lee, another classmate, found a great deal of support in her aunt, Maxine. "Maxine has helped me in a lot of tough situations. She has always been there when I needed her. She taught me how to carry myself. My aunt is like my big sister. She was the one who told me to go back to school. She helped me out when my son was crying and I didn't even know what to do. She was great." Family and friends can sometimes come in the same package.

Syracuse University student Susan Winchester pulled valuable knowledge from the best and the worst in her family situation. "The summer before my freshman year of high school, I came home to find that my father had moved out. I was completely floored—I had never seen my parents fight or even express displeasure with each other. After I got over the shock of feeling left by my father, I turned to my mother for everything. We were best friends. Then in the winter of my sophomore year, before I got over the hope that my parents would get back together, my mother told me that the divorce was going through and that she was going to remarry. Less than two years after my father moved out, I felt that my mother was being taken away also.

"As bleak as the situation was, I would not change the circumstances if given a chance. Of course I still wish that I could have just one week with my parents together in the same house and in love—I will probably never give up that dream, but I have changed so much because of the divorce that I cannot imagine what kind of person I would be otherwise. I have learned that nothing in life is final, and not to count on things remaining static. I do not trust people as easily now, but I also know that if something goes wrong in my life, I shouldn't dwell on it because the situation is salvageable and will definitely change. I have also become more of my own person, and feel that I can achieve anything I put my mind to. If my parents can have the strength to get out of an unhealthy relationship, then I can change an undesirable situation, too. I learned to deal with the problems that occurred that were beyond my control and to take each day in stride."

Teachers and Other Authority Figures

All of you have adults in your lives who are in positions of authority over you; sometimes you gain from those relationships, and sometimes they get on your nerves. Some teachers you love, some you clash with. Some coaches seem to know exactly what you need and how to treat you, and some ignore you. Piano teachers, scout leaders, sponsors of extracurricular activities, parents of your friends—all are part of your life.

Most of the time, people like teachers and coaches are there to help you. They have chosen their professions because they enjoy working with students and helping them reach their potential. If you find you get along well with someone in a position of authority, take advantage of the chance to learn what that person has to teach you and to enjoy the support that comes with a good relationship. Deena Mottola had a teacher who influenced her life profoundly. "I took a non-honors history class my sophomore year because nothing else would fit into my schedule. The teacher really respected me because he could see that I was very serious about learning. He pushed me in a different way— he started me thinking a lot about feminism and the relationships between men and women. He helped me see that if I didn't like the way things were, I didn't have to accept it and I could fight against it. He did this by pushing me to defend my views and giving me a hard time—all in a good-natured way. He made me think and challenged the way I had been thinking."

Even when you initially react negatively to a teacher, you might find that what you learn from that person serves you well later on in your life. Lee Pomeroy gives a formerly disliked teacher a lot of credit. "My tenth-grade English teacher taught us how to read Shakespeare in a very rigorous and systematic way. We all thought it was very difficult and hated it at the time. She made us write a lot of papers and had very high expectations. But after that, I realized I had an appreciation for the beauty of the language that I didn't have before taking her class. Reading literature has opened up new worlds and new experiences and brought a richness to my life. Much of this is thanks to that teacher. If only she knew!"

Paula Bobrowski, a student at Syracuse University, now looks positively at an experience that seemed negative while she was going through it. "Mr. Flangheddy held very high standards. The course was very difficult—the lit book chapters were long, and we were tested on two at a time. We also had to read novels on the side. Every two weeks, we had to finish a novel and then have a quiz or write an expository essay describing things like symbolism or the author's method and relation to society. This experience has had a lot of impact. I no longer enjoy reading as much as I used to, but my writing has definitely improved. And because of the work load, I was forced to prioritize activities and manage my time. I became more respected as a student because of my attitude of preparedness and increased sense of what a real education was all about. At times I struggled and failed, but I came out of the class still an A/B student, ready to face the next challenge."

Some of you are going to have experiences where your chemistry with a certain teacher doesn't click. That's hard—because not only are you turned off by your relationship with that person, you also tend to turn off to the material taught in the class. You may feel that some teachers don't seem to challenge you with the work, or that they don't care about you. You owe it to yourself to do more about this than just to turn off and deny yourself an educational experience. What can you do?

- *You can talk to the teacher.* As unapproachable as some teachers seem, many of them would like to know their students as more than just heads to count in a classroom. They might warm up to you if you come to them outside class and want to talk about how you feel. Do you feel the teacher is giving you too much or too little to do? Do you feel picked on, or ignored, or disliked, and want to know why? Take a chance and ask. Even if the answer ends up being something that doesn't make you happy, at least you know the score. Teachers deal with anywhere from ten to forty different students, at least five times a day—it can be hard under those circumstances for them to tune in to your particular needs. Stand up for yourself and make your needs known, and you have a better chance of having them fulfilled.

- *You can talk to a counselor.* Your school probably has a counselor whose job is to help you with any problems you encounter while in school. If you don't feel comfortable addressing a teacher directly, the counselor might be able to work on the situation. Counselors usually have equitable relationships with teachers and can intercede for you, acting as your agent and working through the problem with the teacher in a less charged environment. Sometimes they can help you see the teacher's perspective better as well.

- *You can see about changing classes.* When your relationship with a teacher makes attending class miserable for both you and the teacher, it might be better if you find a class that still takes care of your academic needs but provides a better environment for you. If your problem with the teacher interferes with your ability to learn, making a change might do you both some good.

Remember that you are responsible for half of what goes into your relationships with those in authority around you. The more you open yourself up to what others want to teach you, the more they will give you. Just as your family members can earn "friend" status, so can your teachers, coaches, and others. As you let yourself get to know people and all their ups and downs and needs and imperfections, whether they are your own age or fifty years older than you, you discover that you can often relate to them on the level of a good friend.

Occasionally a teacher will have the power to turn you around in a memorable way. "Mr. Cooper was our English teacher and also our coach, and he brought out more in me than I ever thought possible," says Edison, New Jersey, native Tom Burdasz. "One time he asked the class to read and analyze a poem. I sat there, eyes fixed firmly on the floor, as the rest of the class read. He marched over to my desk, lifted my chin with his clammy hand, and asked why I wasn't reading. 'I can't,' I said. He fiercely asked me to repeat what I said. 'I can't do this,' I continued, 'because I've always been in the lower-level reading classes.' He slammed his book down and exclaimed, 'Don't you ever say that again. Someone else's opinion of you does not have to be your reality!' He made us realize that anything was possible, in that class as well as in the rest of our lives."

Sometimes, though, you will get stuck with a teacher who is just plain bad, and there is no practical solution to the problem. This happens, and it is not anyone's fault. If you can't apply any of the above solutions to your problem, the best you can do is just stick it out and try to get whatever knowledge you can out of the class material. Focus your energy elsewhere, on some other class or activity that you like, and you'll get through it eventually.

Faraz Haider, a graduate of Corning East High School in New York, has a different perspective on teacher-student relationships. "In the country where I am from, teachers behave like dictators and often give brutal punishments to the students. When I moved to Corning, the atmosphere was completely different. Teachers were cooperative, willing to help, and friendly with the students. I have found that there are very few students who show respect to their teachers. I think teachers deserve a lot of praise for their excellent work—it isn't easy to teach so many students at a time."

Boyfriends and Girlfriends: To Date or Not to Date

One of the big peer pressures in high school for many people is dating. For me, it wasn't that big of a deal, because I never got heavily involved in it. Sure, there were people who I had a crush on, and then there were others who liked me but who I thought of only as friends, even if we dated a little for fun. No one really grabbed my heart, and I didn't think that much about it.

But for many people, the highest highs and lowest lows of high school come from relationships where more than being friends is involved. It's natural to become interested in dating at this point in your life. You are ready to explore the world on a different level, and you are in the time of your life when you are beginning to discover what you will eventually want in a long-term partner. Your curiosity is aroused, and high school with its many social opportunities is a good time to see just what's out there.

What makes a person desirable or attractive to others? Especially at this point in your life, appearance is a major factor. You might also be attracted to people who play certain sports, sing, participate in certain activities, have a great car, or wear the best clothes. But underneath it all, the most crucial factor is self-confidence. If you are confident and self-assured, if you know that you are worth the attention, someone will eventually see that and take note. If you don't yet securely know your worth, your lack of confidence might get in your way.

Heather Pollack didn't really date until she found her niche working at a job that made her happy. "Since I was now doing something [working at the movie theater] that I was very interested in, I became more confident and at ease. Because of this, the boys who worked at the theater, boys who were popular at another high school, started asking me out on dates, and I ended up making a lot of good friends." James Morris found his popularity in a similar way. "I'm involved in two choirs and a band. Music is really important to me; it releases my mind and lets me be free and creative. The band has taught me a lot of things. You have to practice hard to be any good. Our hard work is paying off—we are now starting to play at weddings and other events. Being in a band also makes you very popular with the girls!"

As much as dating can bring fun and learning into your life right now, you certainly won't lack for anything if you don't get into it for a while. Many high school students—more than you might think—date very little or not at all. They might go to formal events like the prom, but they don't go out with each other on a regular basis. You might not feel secure or comfortable going out just yet. You might be too busy with other things. Or you might not know anyone you would want to date. You are not alone!

I have a friend who didn't have one date in high school. She is smart and attractive but just didn't feel comfortable or confident in herself at the time. She thinks people didn't ask her out because she projected that attitude to others around her. In her third year of college, she came into her own and began a relationship with a fellow student that was to last two years. High school just wasn't the right time for her—her "right time" came later, when she felt more sure of herself.

Ryan Walker, a college student from Wayne, Pennsylvania, found out what can happen when the time isn't right to date. "I got to know Nicole in tenth-grade geometry—she sat next to me in the front row. We became really close, talking on the phone and hanging out, and even trusted each other with boyfriend and girlfriend secrets. Then I started to feel this incredible attraction toward her. I fell in love. I couldn't stop thinking about her, and everyone but Nicole knew. After a year of this secret one-sided love affair, I just flat out told her how I felt, over the phone. She was silent for three minutes. Then to make it worse, I wrote her these love poems. We decided to go out on a date to see how she felt—a romantic movie. Bad, bad, bad. We drifted apart for a month and didn't talk at all. She said she didn't know how she felt, and eventually she decided it 'wasn't the right time.' I made a huge fool of myself and lost a good friend."

The pain that you and others can feel when you don't date or don't get invited to parties can be hard to take. But the best way to deal with it is to concentrate on spending time with the people who do care about you. James says, "Pick your friends wisely. Associate with people who have the same values as you do. And don't be worried if you don't have a lot of friends; just having a few who will be there for you is all that you need."

If you don't push it, your dating phase may begin when you least expect it. Gwenan had a big surprise: "The summer before my senior year, I broke my foot and couldn't do ballet for six weeks. This very inconvenient injury caused my social blooming! It started out with everyone in French class signing my cast, more attention than I'd ever received in school. Then, right after my foot healed, I decided to take a risk and tried out for the school musical, *Sweet Charity*. I got the part, and all of a sudden I had this large core of friends. I socialized a lot, went to cast parties, and was very happy. In fact, I even started dating. I was the only one of my original small group of friends to have a prom date!"

Kimberly Buckley, from Sudbury, Massachusetts, is still seeing her high school boyfriend now that she is in college at Syracuse. "I fell in love at sixteen, and he is still the best thing that ever happened to me. I have learned to appreciate my relationship with him as well as my relationships with my family and friends. He has taught me little things, such as how to tell my parents I love them, even when I leave them for a couple of hours. He shares his knowledge with me, from cars to world events, always teaching me something new. I wouldn't have pulled through some of my problems as easily if he were not by my side. He is always there to listen, to laugh with or cry with. He gives support and advice, and I can express myself without worrying about him judging me. Because of him, I now know that to love and be loved are what I want out of life, and that love cannot be searched for—if it is meant to be, it will just happen."

As wonderful as dating may seem, it has its dangers. Taking the chance at the bliss of a relationship involves risking the misery of breakups, fights, miscommunications, and outright lies. Everyone in high school is just learning how to deal with relationships, and learning always involves painful mistakes and difficult experiences. Sarah Lyman Kravits recalls a breakup in tenth grade: "When my boyfriend broke up with me, he said he thought we should still date but see other people. What he meant was that he didn't want to see me anymore; I found that out when he never again asked me out. It took me a long time to stop thinking about him because every time I turned around I would see him flirting with his latest interest in the hallway."

Sometimes a breakup, as painful as it is, can bring rewards. "My boyfriend and I dated for three years, and we were the couple that no one ever could imagine breaking up," says Angela Baldwin, a student from Laurel, Maryland. "When we broke up, I was upset and it was hard, but I am a very strong person and knew it was not the end of the world. Now I know that this experience was one of the best things that could ever have happened to me. Our relationship taught me a lot about myself and relationships in general. Watching something that was part of my life for so long totally diminish taught me a few valuable lessons: I learned that nothing is forever, and I have become more independent. This has made me more down-to-earth and mature. It is too bad that I had to learn the hard way, but I think that is the only way you can learn in these types of cases."

Another danger: some people become so wrapped up in their boy-friend or girlfriend that they lose sight of their own values, opinions, and interests. Some of my friends in high school let their whole worlds revolve around their boyfriends' activities to the point that what their boyfriends thought and did became more important than their *own* thoughts. Plus, they ignored their other friends (including me), and often wondered why they felt left out if they and their boyfriends eventually broke up.

Sometimes this happens when one person becomes possessive of the other person's time and energy. "My freshman year, I went out with this guy for seven months and five days," says Melissa Rekas. "The first five months were great. But then I was in a play and made a lot of friends, some of them guys, and I realized that I never saw them because I was always with my boyfriend. He made it clear that he didn't want me going out with guy friends because he would consider it a date, even though my friends and I wouldn't. He got so possessive—he walked me to and from all of my classes, he was just always there, wherever I was, and became incredibly dependent on me. I was missing out on time with all of my friends, guys and girls both.

"I wanted to break up with him because I felt so stifled, but I couldn't because I felt that I would hurt him too much; he said he would practically die without me. Finally one night I kissed another guy—I didn't really want to even, but it happened, and then I realized that I had to break up with my boyfriend. So I did, and he cried for two days, even in school. It was awful because I still really liked him, but I just couldn't go on that way."

Of course, it's important to spend time together and to be supportive and interested in the person you are dating. Taking an interest in what your boyfriend or girlfriend likes, and doing things together, is the foundation of a good friendship and relationship. But it's risky to give up the essence of your self to be better accepted by a boyfriend or girlfriend. What happens if you break up? What are you left with if you structure your life to fit around another person's desires, activities, or personality? Try to find a balance. If someone cares about the *real you*, they will encourage you to be yourself, make your own choices, and grow in positive directions. They might give advice, but they will recognize the value of your being yourself. Maintain your individuality in relationships. It will provide a foundation for both of you if you stay together, and it will be a source of inner strength if you break up.

The Diverse World: Dealing with Differences

Diversity may or may not be an issue for you in your school. Some high schools are very homogeneous, meaning the students are for the most part similar to one another in culture, race, nationality, or gender. In other schools, you are exposed to people from all types of backgrounds. But no matter what kind of school you go to, you will all eventually move into the mainstream of the world, where different cultures, races, nationalities, genders, levels of ability, and lifestyle preferences exist. Sometimes groups mix and sometimes they keep to themselves, but you are sure to encounter them in your life. Learning to accept and even become close to people who are different from you is an important part of growing up. It's also part of what makes life interesting.

Angela Dorn learned from people both similar to and different from her. An African American, she grew up in a predominantly white community. When her family moved her junior year, she switched to an all-girls high school that had students from all different races and social backgrounds. She got a part-time job that provided her first experience being around a group of people who all shared her racial heritage: "I worked at a McDonald's where all the workers were African-American. At the time I saw it as a kind of 'plantation' in the middle of a totally white suburb. The job itself was awful and I was horrible at it. But in a way it was fun, because it was one of my first exposures to black kids my age."

Dealing with people so different from yourself can take some adjustment, as Angela found out, and success doesn't come easy. "I don't feel like I did a very good job of adjusting when I moved to St. Louis. I moved to a school that was more racially and socially integrated (which I chose for that very reason), but when I got there, I felt a bit of contempt for everyone. I had moved from a wealthy, upper-class, competitive school, and I felt like I was better than everyone else. I see that now as a great failure. I should have risen to the occasion and embraced my new school."

People form groups because they naturally gravitate toward others with whom they have something in common. In a group situation, it's the belonging that is important. Race and culture sometimes stand out and sometimes fade away. If you identify with others who share your race or culture, that is the primary basis of your friendship. If you become friends with someone because you both share an interest, chances are it won't matter if your cultures are similar or not.

There are two keys to minimizing the clashes that occur between different kinds of people. One is to realize that differences are just that—"different," and not "better." We are all immensely different from one another, whether or not you can tell from the outside. Think about your own family. When I was in high school, I felt tons more different from my own brothers than I did from my best friends to whom I was in no way related. I came from the exact same gene pool as my brothers—but I was more in tune with my friends, who were of completely different biological makeups, and often different cultures, races, or traditions, from mine. The ways in which my friends and I were alike made our differences seem unimportant.

Sarah Lyman Kravits is Caucasian and has an African-American friend with whom she has shared and learned a lot: "Chandra and I met because we were both blocked into the same space onstage during a rehearsal for a musical. Ever since then we have called each other 'Half' and have stayed friends for eight years and counting. We have a love for life and dancing and music in common; that brings us together as friends. Then, when we spend time together, we learn from one another's different cultures and traditions. We have grown a lot from opening ourselves up to what is different in each other."

I don't mean to sound as if everything in the diverse world is wonderful and peaceful. Conflict between different groups of people is an all too frequent part of reality. You may see examples of separatism, on a smaller scale, in your school. Some students may not like others or accept them into their cliques because of a cultural difference. Students may reject others who are differently abled (disabled) or who learn in a different way than they do. Many students in high school are threatened by differences and choose to reject them. It can be very painful or anger-producing for those who suffer the rejection. If you are on the receiving end of prejudice or discrimination, the most important thing to do is to maintain your sense of self-worth—even though that can be the hardest thing to do.

Tanaphon Manavutiveth, now at Syracuse University, came to the United States as a high school freshman from Samut Prakan, Thailand. "At my school, every freshman had to participate in an activity called Peer Leadership every Wednesday morning. There I learned how to get along with others in a group and how to cooperate with people I might not like. When I was a junior I became a junior proctor and taught peer leadership to the middle-school students. I was a hall proctor in my senior year, and that job required me to help everybody get along. Many students didn't like each other and wouldn't even talk, and I had to talk to people and change their modes of thinking.

"Having to control people taught me leadership. One of the most important things is to get things to settle down in any kind of fight or emergency situation. There were many fights. I would always suggest that people talk to each other clearly before getting themselves upset. I told them that to get along and communicate with other people is the most important thing, because without that you will not have anything. If you have no friends no one will help you, if no one helps you it's hard to get work, if you have no work you will earn no money, if you have no money you will not have food, and if you have no food you will die."

Sometimes you may find yourself on the other side—the side that uses prejudice against someone else. If so, try to figure out why you wanted to act that way. What need does it fulfill in you? Is it worth causing pain for someone else? Is it fair?

Besides just paying attention to race and culture, stay aware of how you treat people of different economic backgrounds. "There is a tradition at my high school that the senior class divides and each group goes on a four-day retreat," says Broomall, Pennsylvania, native Michael Cellucci, a graduate of St. Joseph's Prep. "Coming from a wide range of diverse backgrounds, students attempt to break down stereotypical walls that have divided the class into cliques. The diversity is so widespread that to one side of you could be the son of a mailman, and to the other side, the son of a brain surgeon. When they get back, the seniors work to set a strong example for the underclassmen.

"This retreat gave me the opportunity to get to know classmates I should have known but didn't because we shared no interests. I'm now more able to get along with many different kinds of people. It has been a lesson in life as well as a help in college; I have had to start over in the friend-making process, and my high school experience taught me to be open and accept everybody for who they are. You never know —you may meet someone your freshman year who is not at all like you and by senior year that person could be your best friend."

One dangerous tradition still exists: sometimes parents and other family members teach children to discriminate and look down on others. Whether adults tell children how to behave or just set an example by behaving a certain way, children pick up on the lesson and make it their own. If you, as a high school student, are beginning to question some of the ideas that you were brought up with, it's important that you find the strength to challenge them. This is a time when you don't take much for granted—you are experimenting with how you want to run your own life. Include prejudicial ideas in the mix of things that you question, and don't forget the golden rule: treat others as you would like them to treat you.

It's important to be proud of who you are. But when being proud hurts someone else, it crosses the line. Try to be a peacemaker in your life. Without abandoning your own heritage, you can open yourself up to other people and to knowledge about cultures and lifestyles different from your own. Your voice can join in the call for peace and acceptance that will help bring our world to a new level of maturity. You can do all that without losing sight of your uniqueness and special talents. Lydia Molina, a high school student in Arizona, says, "I have suffered, like many other people, from discrimination. Even that I don't let get me down. What it makes me do, however, is further my education to show those people that even a 'Hispanic,' like they say, can be as good as they are or even better. That will be the greatest satisfaction that I can have."

· 4 ·

UNCOVERING OPPORTUNITIES
Education Inside and
Outside the Classroom

One of the hippest things Mr. Buchanan taught me was not to play with vibrato in my tone. At first, I used to like to play with vibrato because of the way most of the other trumpet players played the instrument. One day when I was playing in that style, with all this vibrato, Mr. Buchanan stopped the band and told me, "Look here, Miles. Don't come around here with that Harry James stuff, playing with all that vibrato . . . Play straight and develop your own style, because you can do it. You got enough to be your own trumpet man."

MILES DAVIS
Jazz musician
1926–1991

"**V**ibrato" is a musical term used to describe a particular technique of playing an instrument or singing. A vibrato note sounds like two notes alternating with each other, one slightly varied in its pitch. Together they have a single, pulsating sound. It's a technique that has come in and out of style over the years, and when Miles Davis was a senior at Lincoln High School in East St. Louis, in 1944, it was very popular.

But Miles's music teacher at Lincoln had a feeling that this particular student had the power to define his own unique sound. Because Miles had demonstrated that he was serious about his music, Mr. Buchanan was willing to tell Miles what he really thought. It was a helping hand Miles would never forget: not so much because of the advice given, but because of the message behind the advice. It gave Miles a sense of his own importance and talent. He was able to draw strength and encouragement from the fact that someone cared and believed in him.

Areas of Educational Opportunity

Education happens all around you, all day long, whether you are in class or working out with your athletic team, at a part-time job or participating in an internship. Many different resources help you build your knowledge and skills. Since I didn't really apply myself in school until my senior year, I probably missed out on a lot of in-class learning before that time. But without even realizing it, I learned a lot outside class. I learned from what I enjoyed because I opened myself up to it.

School

In the ideal world, education should give you two main things: knowledge of the workings and the capacity of your mind (*how* to learn) and material to build up your storehouse of information (*what* to learn). Learning to use your mind will open a world of options for you, whether you go on to college or directly into the work force. The more you build your knowledge and explore your mind's infinite abilities, the more able you will be to decide which paths suit you and to follow them successfully.

Each of us is born with a powerful mind, but we are then responsible for making the most of its power, taking time and energy to develop, challenge, and broaden it. High school can give you that opportunity, if you choose to take it. Everyone has a different experience, of course, and some people get more out of their high schools than others, because some high schools are more learner-friendly than others and because some students put more effort into seeking out learning opportunities than others do.

Mikah Don Sellers, a business student in Florida who attended Altoona High School in Pennsylvania, talks from his own experience. "I couldn't get into college because my math was so bad, so I had to take all kinds of college prep courses while I was in the navy, and it was a waste of my time and money. If I had paid attention when I was in high school, I never would have had to do that. You've got to take advantage of your education. Make the most of it because once you're out you'll sit there and think, 'I can't get anywhere—I don't know enough about anything!' Pay attention. You can't go back—remember that."

Schools are designed to expose you to all the main branches of learning. When you have taken math and sciences and English and history and languages and arts classes and other electives, two things happen.

For one, you build your knowledge of how you relate to different kinds of information. Your favorite subjects might figure in later when you begin to make a decision about what kind of career you want to pursue.

Two, if you have worked hard enough in your classes, you build your brain power in all kinds of directions. Education is the key to life. The more you know, the more choices are available to you. In the job that I have now in publishing, I use my writing skills when I write proposals and memos and presentations, my reading skills when I read manuscripts and reports and descriptions of books, my math skills when I help to estimate marketing numbers and costs, and my skills in Spanish when I meet with people who work as marketing managers or sales representatives in Spanish-speaking countries.

Maureen Clancy, a student from Clifton Park, New York, took a life lesson from an assigned book. "In eleventh grade I took Literature of Decisions, and we read *The Fountainhead* by Ayn Rand. It was slow going at first, but as we talked about the novel and what it meant to us, it began to get more interesting. It discusses how a person needs to find a career that truly makes them happy—if someone has not made the right career choice, they will be forever unsatisfied. This lesson will continue to affect my decisions for the rest of my life. I will always think about whether the decisions I am making are truly making me happy. I will always remember that true happiness comes from within."

"My most positive experience in high school was my creative writing class," says Syracuse freshman Michael Hobler. "Writing never used to interest me—I pretty much hated every aspect of it. But then I learned to express myself more effectively. I used to be scared to use anything but facts in my papers, but I learned that personal experiences some-times make a paper more effective. My teacher helped me gain confidence by encouraging my personal reflections and telling me that I should write not just to satisfy a teacher but also to satisfy myself. My whole attitude changed—writing became not just something I had to do for school but something of value for my future. I kept a journal for this class—I had to force myself to write in it at first, but I actually found myself enjoying it. I have a special interest in politics, and at the time I was living in Jordan, so it was hard to talk to anyone about politics without getting criticized. My journal was a great escape."

Sometimes your classes will bore you. I've talked about how you can improve your experience by talking to your teachers about it and per-haps even changing classes. But sometimes you might just have to stick it out. Tracy Green Bunch, a college student at the University of Ar-kansas who is at the same time a partner at a real estate company, made a choice that she wasn't so sure about later. "My biggest regret is graduating early. I skipped the eleventh grade because I wanted to get on with my life—I felt like there were better things to be doing than listening to my boring teachers. I missed out on the fun of my senior year because I was in a hurry. My advice is to take your time and enjoy high school. I also dealt with my energy by riding and competing on horseback. Find something you enjoy—horses were hard to get bored with because I never knew what to expect. I guess any sports are like that—you never know exactly what to expect."

What do *grades* mean? Of course, it's important to do well in class. But consider your classwork as something you do to improve yourself and your mind power, not just a way to have good grades to show to parents and college admissions officers. Good grades that don't have much solid learning and hard work behind them are pretty empty— when you get out into the real world, grades disappear, and it's your abilities that really count.

Grades should be a *product* of your hard work in class, not the focus of it. The point should be to learn for your own growth and development, but that often gets lost in the jungle of expectations and pressures from parents, friends, college recruiters, and others. Focusing too hard on grades for their own sake or to make other people happy can mean trouble. James Morris says, "My family put a lot of pressure on me to do well in school. Sometimes when I was growing up I felt like I made straight A's for my mom and played football for my uncle. I really rebelled against the family pressure when I was a freshman, and I let my grades slip. Now I know that it is very important to do things for myself—I'm doing well because I want to for myself and no one else."

When you receive a grade that you feel is unfairly low, take some time to think about it. It may indeed be unfair, and in that case you should talk to your teacher. On the other hand, it may indicate something important about whether you have learned something properly. Brooke Davis of Bryn Athyn, Pennsylvania, found out how grades can sometimes indicate exactly what you have learned. "I had always gotten relatively good grades through high school, but that streak of easy A's ended the spring of my senior year. I was taking a course called Great Books, and we were about to take the essay exam on *How Green Was My Valley*. I had somewhat paid attention in class, but only to my teacher, not my classmates. My teacher was good but had a unique style: he would start the class by saying something completely wrong and then wait for the class to respond and contradict him. I glanced over my notes the night before the test and decided that I was ready.

"When it was time for the test, I selected one essay from our choice of ten and wrote for the entire period. I wasn't extremely proud of it, but I thought I would get my usual high grade. When we got the papers back, I had to look at my grade twice. Not only had I not gotten the expected A, I had failed the test. When I went to talk to my teacher, he pointed out a few technical errors, then proceeded to tell me that I had answered the question wrong because I had answered solely based on what he said and hadn't paid attention to my classmates' comments. I was angry at my teacher because I felt tricked. After mulling it over for a few days, I realized that my grade wasn't my teacher's fault—it was mine. I hadn't paid enough attention to my peers. Although I failed that test, I learned a very valuable lesson: the importance of listening to others all the time."

Take a look at how you feel about school. What are your favorite classes?

_____

_____

_____

Your least-favorite classes?

_____

_____

The time you spend in a classroom represents only a small fraction of your life. By giving you the basics, your teachers can plant the seeds. Then it's your turn to put in the work that gets those seeds to take root and bear fruit. Mikah advises, "Push your teachers. They don't know what you want sometimes, so you have to tell them what you need. Let your teachers know you as a person."

Extracurricular Activities

After-school activities can provide all kinds of educational experiences for you. You can learn from what you do, from working with other people, and from simply dedicating yourself to something and having the discipline to work on it for a certain number of hours each week. You can learn about the *kinds* of activities you like as well. Are you

into the hard-driven physicality of football? The creativity and camaraderie of the drama club? The strategy of the chess club? The finesse
of soccer or field hockey? The stamina of cross-country or the speed of
sprinting? Or even the variety of the language clubs?

ATHLETIC TEAMS/SPORTS

Sports can give you pride in yourself and your team for working hard,
a sense of belonging to a group of people, appreciation for cooperation,
and the fun of representing your school in game situations. You don't
have to be the biggest or most muscle-bound person in the world to
participate. "Football takes a great deal of commitment and work," says
James Morris. "I have to keep a 2.7 GPA to stay on the team. I'm not
as big as the other players, and so I have to rely on my mind and my
intelligence to play well, not just my physical strength. Last year we
went to the city championships, which made me very proud."

Teamwork is one of the biggest parts—and the biggest benefits—of
playing any sport. Syracuse University freshman Joanne Ebeling credits
her athletic experience with teaching her how to function as a team
member. "Teamwork is a very important part of basketball. In order
to win games, you need all five players to work together and contribute.
You have to be willing to pass the ball to everyone, and to get along
with everyone on the court. Basketball actually helped me meet people."

Sarah Lyman Kravits went out on a limb and joined the field hockey
team her sophomore year. "I was taking five dance classes a week, so
I was in good shape, but I felt out of touch with my school. I wanted
to connect with people outside of class. Since field hockey didn't really
require any prior experience, I tried out and made the JV team. My
parents were worried that I didn't have the time to do it, and my dance
teacher was angry because she thought the running I'd be doing would
hinder my progress in dance class. But it was so important to me to
feel connected to my high school that I stuck with it through senior
year. I did have less time to socialize during field hockey season and
had to work harder to keep up in class, but it was worth it to feel like
I belonged everywhere and to represent my school. One year our hard-
fought games and tough practices paid off in a county championship
and regional final."

That kind of determination can get you involved in a sport—and it
can also grow as you continue to participate, as Huntingdon Valley,
Pennsylvania, native Jason Kovar found out. "Determination was an
immense lesson I learned from football. Not only does working hard
three hours a day, six days a week, start to take a toll on your body,

your mental state also begins to get a little shot. This is when you have to say to yourself, don't let yourself down, and don't let the people around you down. Anyone can play the game in front of hundreds of people, but it takes determination to work hard enough behind closed doors where no recognition is given. You have to be determined to make things happen."

Sports can help you discover things about yourself even if you have never been an especially athletic person. "I played JV and varsity basketball," says Jim Lindsey. "It was challenging and fun even though I was never one of the top players. I hadn't done much athletically before, and it taught me that I could enjoy sports. I still really love basketball and play occasionally." Dominic Ciresi counts baseball as one of his favorite things in life. "When I first started playing, I wasn't a star player at all. That taught me humility! I learned to work closely with people who were better than me and how to 'fill in' where I could. It taught me that in sports, as is often the case in life, the welfare of the team is the highest goal. I'm still planning to play intramural baseball at Northwestern, and I coach Little League in the summer."

NON-ATHLETIC EXTRACURRICULARS

Valuable experiences can be found off the playing fields as well. Yearbook was one of my big activities in high school. I got into it because my friend Madeline had been a member of the staff and told me I would like it, and also because I wanted to become involved in something that was ongoing and not just a one-shot, one-day deal. I didn't feel I had a skill (like writing) that would allow me to be on the newspaper staff, so the yearbook was the next best thing.

Although working on the yearbook staff was not one of the most exhilarating experiences I had in high school, it taught me a lot. I learned about layout and design; I learned to work on stories with photographers; I interacted with people who were different from me—quieter, more studious and focused. I always looked forward to fifth period because it was a time to be creative with stories and photographs and people who liked to put them all together to portray our high school experience.

Katy O'Connor just graduated from high school in East Sandwich, Massachusetts, where she was active as a cheerleader. "I developed many leadership roles in my four-year involvement with cheerleading. I gained the courage to cheer and dance in front of a large crowd two or three times a week. I was elected captain of the squad in eleventh grade, which was a great responsibility, because many people depend on you and your actions. Being a captain taught me how to work with others more efficiently—I had to teach routines, organize practices, handle problems with other cheerleaders, and maintain control so that everyone would listen to me and respect me. Also, the teamwork that I developed helped me in the classroom and on the court and field. No matter how frustrating some situations became, we could work efficiently with each other and were able to perform an excellent routine."

The arts offer learning opportunities as well. After three years of watching others sing onstage, Gavin Carrier, from Apalachin, New York, decided to try himself. "I used to criticize people for letting fear ruin their performances. But in my senior year, it was time to stop talking and to walk the walk. So I signed up for the talent show, and there I stood in the stage lights with four hundred people staring at me. I could feel the pressure in the air. I had to stand and sing this song, which made me feel almost naked in front of everyone. When I belted out the first lyrics, I heard myself not doing well—and then the fear of not achieving overcame the stage fright. My voice came back and I let it go. As the song ended, I knew I had done well. The cheers made me feel ten feet tall. This experience showed me that if you don't worry about what others think and just do it, you will succeed."

High schools offer so many other activities that give you a chance to get involved: language clubs, dance clubs, cheerleading or drill teams, math or chess or academic teams, writing clubs, theater and singing and instrumental music groups, computer clubs, and more. Finding out what you might like and joining up helps you feel you are part of the action. Maybe you don't know anyone involved in the activities you want to try—but since you know that the people involved share your interests, you already have something in common. Look for something that interests you, and give it a try. It's not a job—if you don't like it, you can move on to something else. Give yourself the chance to learn from something other than your classwork.

If nothing offered seems to interest you, consider starting your own group or activity! That's what Deena Mottola did. "I helped a friend start a Teen Crisis Hot Line in our school library. We chose a group of our friends who would help us, and we would hang around the school at night taking phone calls. Kids from the area would call with parental problems, problems with girlfriends or boyfriends, etc. We heard a lot of interesting stories! It was nice to think we were helping people, but it was also a lot of fun to hang out at night with my friends."

List your favorite school activities here:

_____

_____

_____

Put down one you think you might want to try—then look into it!

_____

Working Part-time

These days many high school students need to work because of tight family budgets. A part-time job can be valuable to you, and not just in terms of money. Work is all about responsibility! It can teach you how to be on time, how to accomplish tasks, how to follow rules and instructions given to you by your boss, and how to work cooperatively with others. And when the paycheck comes, it can teach you how to budget your money effectively.

When I turned sixteen and could legally work, I decided to end my career as a baby-sitter and look for a real part-time job. My first road-block was my parents, who didn't want me to work just yet, even though my brothers had each worked at sixteen. This was one of the first times I noticed that my parents treated me differently because I was a girl, and I was bound and determined that I would not be denied this important rite of passage.

I planned to look for a job as a hostess or, if that failed, in retail at the mall. So I spent my birthday cruising from one restaurant to another, and later that day, after filling out about twenty applications, I arrived at the Spaghetti Company. I had a half-hour interview with the manager, who asked about school mostly—how I had done, what I liked to study, what activities I participated in—and my work history, and after talking with the headwaiter she gave me the job.

I was nervous my first few days and I made some mistakes, like seating people in a closed section and giving one waiter more people than he could handle. But over time I became comfortable with the job and the people and really began to enjoy my work. One of the hardest lessons was learning how to deal with the other hostesses, who knew each other and didn't welcome me as a new member of the team. They gossiped and whispered and acted petty. Instead of trying to fit in, I decided to ignore them and focus on doing a really good job, which pleased my manager. It's best not to let people get to you. If you can be polite to someone even when they are jealous or rude, you can keep your dignity and not sink down to their level.

I looked for a job in order to have independence and spending money, and I was lucky enough to find one that filled the bill without taking too much time away from my other obligations, such as family and homework. When you want a job, think about your reasons why, and try not to compromise other important areas of your life. If you work at a good-paying job because you or your family needs the extra cash but it puts your grades in jeopardy, you may make money but you deny yourself the education that will help you earn more money later on. Or if the hours that you work at a job take away all of the time that you spend with the people in your life, the extra spending money alone may not be worth it. Look at all the possible trade-offs and make sure that you attend to your other commitments on some level while holding down a job.

Some people manage to find a job in an area that interests them. Becky Amato found work using her language skills. "I worked as a teacher's aide at a Hebrew school during high school and I ended up teaching the class. I found the work very satisfying because I liked working with kids and enjoyed having them look to me for guidance. I was also proud to be proficient in a language so few other people knew. My experience made me feel so good that sometimes I think I might still like to be a teacher."

More often than not, you just want to find any job that brings in some money and gives you experience. Gwenan Wilbur had some good and bad feelings about her job. "During my senior year, I worked at a movie theater. It was the first time I realized that men and women are often given different jobs. The men got to do the interesting jobs, selling tickets, running the projectors. The women basically got to clean out the popcorn machine and bathrooms. But the good thing was that I finally had money of my own. That was a wonderful feeling. I could buy the clothes I wanted and finance my new social life. In this respect, my job was very important to me."

Any kind of work that you take provides experience, lessons to learn, and money to spend or save. Whether you teach day care, sell hamburgers, wait tables, ring up jeans and sweaters at a clothing store, or pump gas, your experiences add to your knowledge of the world.

Internships and Co-ops

When you take an internship, you volunteer your work in exchange for the privilege of learning a skill or trade and making connections with people in an industry rather than for a salary.

John Torrente, a teaching student from New Jersey, stumbled upon an internship opportunity that changed his life. "At my high school, we had homeroom at the start of each day—twelve minutes of 'downtime' when we slept, laughed, crammed for tests, and talked about girls. One day when I halfheartedly read the day's announcements, I saw a request for volunteers to work at a camp for the handicapped. I figured I had better things to do, but the camp was still on my mind at the end of the day. The next day I slipped away from my usual raucous lunch table to get more information at Guidance (I didn't really talk about it, since it wasn't cool to go to Guidance). Two weeks later I was there, at a summer camp for the handicapped. I wondered what I was doing there—all my friends were at the shore, in summer school, or cruising around town. But as I look back, I am convinced that my internship at the camp gave me direction in my career, understanding about the working world, and inspiration that I could accomplish something. I realized there that I wanted to spend my life helping people."

The morning announcements led to an internship for Cicero, New York, native Dan Austin as well. "One day there was a call for those interested in interning at a college radio station. I decided it might keep me active that summer, so I sent an application. I was accepted, and after my first meeting a few weeks later I was hooked! The entire summer I spent more than twenty hours a week involved in almost all departments of the station. By the end of it I was July Staffer of the Month and had spent so much time in radio that I began to see it as a career option. Since then I chose my university because it was known as a premier school for mass media, and I was hired as a part-time air personality because of my previous experience. I now see how one decision in one moment can change the course of your life. Others always told me that the key to success lay in being willing to discover new things and try new activities, and now I agree."

A co-op program is when you spend some of your time in school and some of your time working, usually scheduled so that both school and work get equal time. For example, the co-op students at Seward Park High School in New York City work full-time for a week and then go to school for a week, and so on. A co-op program gives you the chance to work more than the average student can while still staying involved in school, although it often takes more time to finish school than it takes for people who are in school full-time. It's a great opportunity for students whose financial needs require them to work more than just part-time. Sometimes students have a tough family money situation or have children of their own to support; in a co-op they can earn the money they need while still continuing to pursue the education that will help them move up in the world later on.

Sara Banker, from Scotch Plains, New Jersey, worked in a senior project that, like a co-op program, took her out of school for a few weeks. "I worked with National Marketing Services, a company that stocks shelves in various stores nationwide. The project took me from the lowest position in the company all the way to the top. I was exposed, hands on, to what goes on day-to-day in many different aspects of the business. First I did manual labor in Toys 'R' Us stores—pulling boxes from the storage room, checking the floor plans to make sure there was enough space, and laying the toys on the shelves. I learned that presentation makes a drastic difference in sales. After that I worked in the NMS offices, doing filing, mailings, and other secretarial work. Finally I moved up to the executive position. I sat in on a business meeting, helped supervise a team in a Toys 'R' Us, and spent a day with the president of NMS. My experiences will stay with me and benefit me as I begin my higher education in business management."

Human Resources

What Miles Davis learned in high school was the secret most successful people understand. To really get what you want in life, to get the most out of yourself, you have to learn how to benefit from the wisdom of others and to take advice from them. Furthermore, you're going to have to be able to sift through what you're told by all the people who advise you (and there will be many) and to know whose advice to trust. There will be times when advice does not fall right into your hands—and those times will be when you'll have to know how to get the advice that's really going to help you. While life decisions are ultimately yours alone to make, there are plenty of potential advisers out there upon whom you can rely for help.

Advice turned things around for Cynthia Nordberg. "Although I planned to go to college after high school, for some reason I couldn't do it—it seemed impossible. So I got a job. I was a secretary for account executives at a stock market firm. It was fast-paced and I learned a lot, but I knew it was a dead-end position—I couldn't be promoted without an education. My boss was a no-nonsense kind of guy. After I'd worked with him for a year, he pulled me aside one day and asked, 'What are your future plans?' I really didn't have any. He said, 'A person like you should be in college. You've got what it takes to do anything you want. Why work for a broker when you can be one?' Later we had lunch and talked some more. His confidence in me gave me the courage I needed to tackle college and earn my degree. As a professional now myself, I seek to pass on to the young people I work with the same blessing he gave to me."

Some of you may feel that it is "weak" to accept advice from others. You may feel much more proud doing things your own way and making your own decisions, no matter what. But don't let that pride prevent you from listening to, and following, advice that could save you a lot of trouble.

Counselors and Advisers

Your counselors are paid to spend time gathering information that can help you and making sure to pass that information on to you. They can help you with everything from college applications to problems with students and/or teachers to academic troubles to making decisions about which class to take or which activity or group to join.

Maybe you haven't ever been to the counselor's office, but don't feel shy about going. In my school, some students had the idea that going to the counselor was for people who had mental problems, and they avoided making the trek. But counselors are there for everyone, no matter what the question or problem. If you are hesitant about making an appointment, you can do it over the phone or through the front office.

All counselors are different, or course. Some will be very forthcoming with information that can help you. Some will be less talkative, waiting to hear what you have to say. You may or may not feel as if you "click" with your particular counselor. If you don't feel helped, you can do a couple of things. If your school has more than one counselor, try seeing another in the hope that you will feel more comfortable. Or be more aggressive when you meet with the counselor. Mikah Don Sellers felt he should have been more demanding when he sought a counselor's aid. "If you don't really know what you need or what you are feeling, which happens a lot, ask the counselor to help you figure it out. When I went to see my counselor, he asked me, 'What do you need to know?' And I thought to myself, 'Well, I'm sixteen, I don't have any idea what

I want to ask or what I want to know! You tell me!' But I didn't say it, and I should have."

Your counselors at school can also be a big help to you as you work through college applications or career planning. They can walk you through the college application process and/or get you started thinking about careers in which you might be interested. If vocational training is what you have in mind, they'll be able to help you with that, too.

Counselors serve a lot of students! If you let your counselors get to know you personally, they will be better able to help you. When they understand your particular interests and goals, they might think of you when they come across material or ideas that might help you. Ask them questions. It is their job to be up-to-date about resources that might help you—career programs, other kinds of counseling, internships, summer jobs, scholarships, work-study programs, and more.

Role Models

"One night in January of my freshman year, I came home from school and found out that my father had lost his job," says Jessica Riese, a graduate of Pingree School and a native of Wilmington, Massachusetts. "He explained that the company had not been sufficiently profitable. I didn't understand why my father was chosen to suffer this humiliation. He is a hard worker and a very intelligent man with a family to support. During his unemployment, my father attended workshops, rewrote his résumé, and applied for jobs. He went to support groups with other unemployed people, consulted to make extra money, and taught a computer course at the state unemployment office. I admire his strength during this terrible time. He was frustrated sometimes by the lack of results from his hard work, but he did not lose hope, even after months of interviewing. Finally, after a year, he was offered a position.

"During my first year at Pingree, I was extremely depressed. The transition from public to private school was overwhelming. Taking notes, class discussions, and the pressure of essay tests were new to me. When I didn't meet my standards—straight A's—I was disappointed and discouraged. That was when I began to realize that the way my father handled his situation had a big effect on me. Although he faced many disappointments, he did not give up. He was my role model. To this day, whenever I find myself frustrated at school, I still reflect on my father's strength, and it helps me realize my potential."

Role models are human resources because they give you a blueprint for how you can accomplish things in your life. It's hard to know how

to achieve the things that you want—you often know where you want
to be but don't have any idea of the first step.

Dave Case, an actor from Chicago who now works in Los Angeles,
found a role model in a Russian director with whom he worked. "This
guy poured his heart and soul into what he did—directing—and
through his example I learned to commit myself to what I wanted to
do as well. He always said that you should treat what you love to do
like a Picasso—put your energy into it, guard it, care about it—and
your commitment will get you to where you want to be."

"My role model is my Aunt Betty Ross," says Chicago high school
student Shaun Crawford. "She's always been there for me. My mother
has had a drug problem most of her life, so Bet took me in when I was
a baby. She didn't have to do it, but she did. She likes to have fun,
and she pulls everyone in on the fun, too. I also like how she treats
everybody the same. I know she loves me, but she also loves other
kids in our neighborhood. She knows how to say things in a nice way
and still get her point across. I want to be like that. And she's never
made excuses for me. If I'm wrong, she'll agree with my boss or teacher
if they've called her in to talk about me. To me, a good role model is
someone who walks their talk. My aunt fusses a lot, and she makes
me really mad sometimes. But as I get older, I'm glad she's kept after
me. I wouldn't be where I am today without her inspiration and the
example she sets."

Role models can be people you know or people you only know about.
There are stories all around you, in the paper, on TV, in magazines,
and in your neighborhood, of people who have set examples for others
who want to be just as honorable, strong, hardworking, caring, and
successful as they are. Do you admire the drive of President Bill Clinton,
the intelligence of actor Alfre Woodard, the tenacity of athlete Bo Jack-
son, or the caring nature of human rights activist Audrey Hepburn?
Take a look around and see who's sitting where you want to be someday; then find out how they got there.

Mentors

Mentors are like superinvolved role models. Not only are they examples
of things you want to be and do, they are also part of your life, friends
who stand by you and advise you whenever you need guidance. Since
mentors know you personally, they will give you advice specifically
directed to your particular problem or concern. Their advice comes from
the knowledge they have built up through the many experiences they

have had. Through them, you can benefit from that knowledge without having to go through the experiences yourself.

MENTOR, noun.
1. a wise and dependable counselor
2. a person who gives advice and direction based on experience or knowledge

---

Mentors can offer advice, support, a shoulder to cry on, encouragement, special opportunities to learn, experiences you wouldn't have had otherwise, and perspective when you are trying to make a tough decision. They can sometimes help you open up a side of yourself that you couldn't see on your own. Jim Lindsey says, "I had an art teacher that I admired and became friends with. Before I met him, I didn't really know myself artistically. He was a positive, friendly man who encouraged and challenged the artistic side of me and expected me to have a lot of discipline. He left the school while I was still there, but then he allowed me to come to Washington, where he had moved, to do a senior project with him. I spent a couple of weeks doing etchings and drawings full-time like a real artist would. Although I don't draw much anymore, he really influenced me and helped me develop an artistic sensitivity."

A mentor can be anyone you choose. In the school environment, a teacher you like and get along with is an ideal candidate. Special relationships with teachers don't come along every day. You won't "connect" with all of your teachers, but probably one or two seem special to you. Maybe you enjoy what they teach, or how they run the class, or you just get a sense that they care about you. What should you do? Cultivate the relationship by seeking teachers out before or after class. Let them get to know you. Ask questions about your homework, or something that was mentioned in class. Try especially hard to do well for them. Let them see that you're giving their class your best.

Dominic Ciresi found a mentor in one of his teachers at boarding school. "My Russian teacher was particularly influential in my life. She was dynamic and accessible because her office was in our dormitory. We spent a lot of time just hanging out with her after school talking about Russian and all sorts of other things. In class, we could speak up and say whatever we wanted. Sometimes she even let me teach class, which really gave me a feeling of confidence and empowerment. I enjoyed it so much that I might want to be a teacher."

Some of you might feel that getting close to your teachers will brand you a teacher's pet. That may be true, but if your relationship with your teacher is important to you, it will outweigh any ribbing you might take from your friends. Put yourself first. If you get something valuable from having a teacher as a mentor, guard that relationship no matter what. Friends who tease you might just be insecure or jealous. Friends who don't are the people who are truly worth your time. If it really bothers you, just seek out your teachers on your own time. No one has to know.

Jeff Lockwood, my physics teacher, was a kind of mentor to me. I had about zero aptitude in physics, but between Mr. Lockwood and my lab partner I muddled through with a C, and later worked my way up to a B. Mr. Lockwood helped me understand that even though I didn't take naturally to physics I was still a smart person with a lot to offer. It is easy to feel done in by any kind of defeat, academic or athletic or whatever, and it takes someone who cares about you to show you that you have unique and valuable qualities elsewhere. I consider Mr. Lockwood one of the real heroes of my education because he could inspire within me the very best I had to offer.

Teachers aren't the only mentors around. Parents, friends, relatives, and other authority figures can be mentors as well.

If you have parents who are a strong presence in your life, probably no one cares for you more than they do. Garth Kravits has always considered his father one of his most important mentors: "My father always made it clear that I could come to him for anything and not be judged. He lets me be myself but guides me and tells me things he sees happening in me, or potential things that I could do, before I see them myself. I ask him for advice on finances, love, my career, anything that comes up. He is always there for me one hundred percent." Even though many people become somewhat separated from their parents during the teen years, often parents still want to help. If you have a problem or a question and aren't sure where to turn, try your parents.

For those of you who have a difficult relationship with your parents, or no relationship at all, think of other people who have taken a parental *role* in your life. Perhaps you are close to a grandparent, an aunt or uncle, or a stepparent. Or maybe you have always felt more comfortable with a neighbor or a parent of a friend of yours. Tamika Leslie found a mentor outside her home: "My mentor is Nadine. I met her in my school program, Mitsui Mentor Program. She helped me prepare my résumé so that I could get a job. She took the day off to take me shopping for an interview outfit and prepared me for the interview by asking questions they would ask. I got the job, and I don't think I could have done it without her."

James Morris found a mentor within his family circle: "One of my mentors is my godbrother. Even though we are the same age, I really respect him and look up to him. When he came to my high school, he handled himself really well—he performed to the best of his ability in sports, made lots of friends, and stayed out of the gangs. I admire the way he conducts his life, and he has helped me follow his example."

Can a friend also be a mentor? Sometimes. As you are probably well aware, most of our friends are all too willing to give us advice: "I can't believe you're wearing those pants." "Nobody does their hair that way." The challenge is to figure out if that advice comes from someone who really has your best interests at heart. If friends happen to be your age, and have had more or less the same experiences you've had, they might not take the same kind of interest in you that a mentor would. They want to be friends, not to put the kind of energy into supporting you and encouraging you in your goals that a mentor can. Lots of times they are just as much in the dark as you are.

Friends who are older often stand a greater chance of becoming mentors for you, since they can more easily give you the wisdom of their experience, and you can more easily respect that wisdom because of the age difference. Carol Gray, an upperclassman at my high school in Tucson, became a kind of mentor for me when I tried out for song leading—a kind of drill-team group that performed dances to music at sports events. She took an interest in me for some reason—maybe because I reminded her of herself at the same age. She helped me practice and really encouraged me. When I didn't make it, she was there to console me and help me feel better. Whenever I saw her at school, I felt good, because she took a genuine interest in me. I knew she believed in me, and that made a real difference in how I felt about myself. We stayed friends throughout college despite our three-year age difference.

Some of you might not be in the habit of seeking out advice. Although you can make your way on your own, it can be a lot easier if someone else gives you a leg up. There isn't anything quite like the wisdom that comes from someone who has "been there." Even though you will learn most concretely through your own experience, the advice you get is that road map which can help you find your way across the unfamiliar terrain of life.

If you want to find a mentor, think about the people you admire and respect in your life. Think about who makes you feel special or important or worthy of attention. Then make the effort to further your relationships with those people. Seek them out for advice or just for conversation. They might be flattered by your respect and respond by opening up to you even more. Mentoring relationships usually evolve from bonds that have started to form naturally. It's hard to gauge who will be a mentor for you, and it's hard to create that relationship where nothing existed before. Dominic Ciresi had a mentor program at his school where each student was assigned a "mentor" from the faculty, but he didn't feel that was fertile ground for mentoring: "They were selected for us and helped us choose classes, but I didn't consider that person a 'real' mentor, and even though he helped me, I wasn't especially inspired by him."

You won't always follow the advice you receive from your mentors. Sometimes your own instincts will go against that advice, and that's fine. You always have the final decision about your own life, and you should never be expected to take anyone's word for gospel. But know that, for the most part, mentors and counselors give advice that they have learned through *their own mistakes*. Their attempt to help you often comes from a desire that you not suffer through what they had to endure. If they are smart, they will offer advice while still recognizing that you need to make your own way.

■ PART TWO ■

EXPLORING YOUR WORLD

· 5 ·

BALANCING YOUR PRIORITIES AND SETTING GOALS
Identifying What You Want and Planning How to Get It

How long can I keep at it? How many more chances will I have to accomplish what I haven't, most importantly to take my team to the World Series, make the catch, hit the game winner that wraps it up? Some may want it as much as I. No one wants it more.

DAVE WINFIELD
Major league baseball player
Born 1951

In 1992, in his nineteenth season, forty-one-year-old Dave Winfield achieved his most important goal: winning the World Series. On the way to that goal, he also became the oldest player in the history of the Major Leagues to amass more than 100 RBI (runs batted in) in the regular season. It was an inspiring achievement that drew standing ovations wherever Dave played. The fans admired not only his success but the perseverance he had shown, year after year, since his career began back in 1973. They knew that he was a winner, and that the road had not been easy.

Whether you are a baseball fan or not, you know that winning it all doesn't come overnight. The goal, for Dave Winfield, had been set many years earlier at Central High in St. Paul, Minnesota. There he learned the importance of commitment, dedication, and hard work. Before his senior year, he was named to the All-State squad, and led his own high school team (as both a shortstop and a pitcher) to the

83

state championship. Dave also valued a solid education. He was drafted by the Baltimore Orioles when he was still seventeen and in high school, but he turned the offer down, knowing that he would have even more options for success if he stayed in school until he graduated and continued to practice and develop his talent.

He enrolled at the University of Minnesota on a partial scholarship, living at home with his mother to keep costs down. In addition to his athletic pursuits, Dave majored in African-American studies and political science. He made the Dean's List and earned a scholarship honor based on his excellence in both athletics and academics. By the time he graduated, Dave had greatly expanded his options. He was drafted by the San Diego Padres as a baseball player, by the Atlanta Hawks as a basketball player, and by the Minnesota Vikings as a football player (even though he had never played a single game of football). Dave stuck with his goal of becoming a baseball star and used his education to figure out how to help others. In 1977 he founded the David M. Winfield Foundation to provide assistance to disadvantaged kids.

Dave Winfield is a prime example of someone who figured out what his values were, set goals with those values in mind, prioritized his goals, and managed his time so that he could achieve as much as possible. Even though it sounds as if he is some kind of superman, he struggled a lot as he pushed his way to the top. As tough as it is to decide what matters most to you in life, it's even harder to dedicate your energies to those ideals and goals. But it pays off when you find yourself where you always wanted to be.

Defining Your Values

Developing your own thoughts and ideas about what you believe in defines your identity just as your talents and personal qualities do. It's good to stand back from the crowd and ask yourself: What's important to me? What do I *value*? What do I believe in?

VALUE, verb.
  to think highly of, esteem
VALUES, noun (plural).
  principles, goals, or standards

Your exact personal definition of values can be difficult to pin down, can take a long time to form (even years), and may change often. Values are the intangibles that make life meaningful, like family, special friendships, a certain job, the desire to volunteer, a spot on an athletic team or the student council. Values define what is important to you.

One of the most important values I learned in high school was the value of life itself. My grandmother, in her nineties at the time, lived with us, and I took care of her during my junior and senior years of high school. Although her mind was sharp, she was becoming gradually weaker physically. She needed help to get to the bathroom, to the family room, and to bed. As I spent time with her on Friday nights so my parents could go out, I thought about how strange it must be for her to need me to take care of her. She had lost her husband after eight years of marriage, raised three kids during the Depression, and became a nurse in her seventies. In what seemed like no time at all, this woman whose life once stretched out before her was now at the end of her days. The experience taught me how precious and fleeting life is—I came to value it and to take care not to waste it at any cost.

Parenthood defined not one but two values for Tamika Leslie. "My son is the most important thing in my life. When I had him, I stopped going to school for a while. I decided that it was time for me to go back to school when he started walking and getting older. I decided that school is as important as my son, because without school I can't give my son the life I want him to have."

ETHICS, noun.
  a code of principles, standards, or habits with respect to right or wrong in conduct; can belong to a particular person, religion, group, or profession

---

Ethics help us make all kinds of decisions, big and small, from how to talk to a parent to whom to date to how to spend time in the evenings. Your ideas about what is right and what is wrong make up your system of ethics. For instance, I had already heard the message that drugs were wrong from parents and other authority figures. But just being told never has the same power as actually seeing or experiencing something that brings the idea home.

When I was in high school, pot never seemed like a big deal to me —I had no interest in it. But I began to see the downside of pot and other drugs in people I knew. It seemed to me that the people who avoided or stopped using drugs were able to move on in their lives, go to college, and/or get good jobs. They had options and could make choices. But friends who didn't ever outgrow the drug phase went on to dead-end jobs that don't provide much financial future. They stayed static, never progressing toward goals or achievements, hiding from the world and disconnecting from others. I didn't like what I saw, and it helped me form part of my ethical code.

Both values and ethics are specific to each individual, although people can share similar values or accept the same code of ethics. Values and ethics come from many different sources: family members, the media (TV, movies, reading material, radio), friends, teachers and other authority figures, religious teaching, and even individual life experiences. When you are young, you tend to accept what others tell you to believe. But now that you are a more responsible and independent individual, you can define your own beliefs. As you explore them, you can add to existing ones, discard ones that no longer make sense to you, and keep those that prove worthy.

When Jim Favicchio of Coxsackie, New York, lost his dad, he gained a strong knowledge of his own values. "My brother passed away at the young age of sixteen when I was only in the eighth grade, and my father passed away when I was in the tenth grade. He was fifty-six years old. Everyone worried that I would take a turn for the worse when all this happened, but I proved them wrong. My father always emphasized the importance of a good education, so in his honor I became a student dedicated to my schoolwork. I hope that my father and brother are watching me work to make them proud. My main objective in life is to become the man my father was: intelligent, caring, unselfish, and the world's greatest dad."

Eve Sangenito of Port Jefferson, New York, also learned from a death in her family. "My grandfather died of cancer of the liver. I never could have expected it, because he was such a strong man, not only physically, but strong-willed. He had served in World War II and raised four children on his own while pursuing a forty-year career in engineering. I was in awe hearing stories about him. When we went to his house to settle his things, I feared being there without him, but actually it gave me comfort to go through his personal memorabilia and think about him. I vividly remember saying goodbye to him. I stood beside the coffin and stared at him—he looked like a different person, because I saw him from a different perspective. He wasn't just my grandpa, he was a man, a father, and a friend to many. This picture will be inside my heart forever, reminding me to appreciate, to love, and to value the most special aspect of my life—my family."

Although life-and-death issues teach enduring lessons, other less earth-shattering events can inspire you to change. For example, the subject of cheating raises ethical issues, issues that Justin Meitzer found himself having to consider. "I was at an all-boys boarding school in New England. All through high school I was a diligent worker, and one night when I was studying for my algebra exam, one of my friends came in with a copy of the exam. In a split-second decision, I grabbed the exam and copied down some of the problems. This action went against my accomplishments and my morals, but nothing stopped me. I went into the exam the next day with sweaty palms, knowing I was about to break a major school rule. The proctor approached me midway through and asked me if I cheated, and I was up front with him and told him that I had. He asked me to leave and took my exam.

"When I was called to see the headmaster after lunch, I discovered that I had made a big mistake. I had to meet with him, teachers, some students on school council, and the deans. I told them exactly what happened, because I knew that if I were dishonest again, it would have created a bigger problem. The committee decided not to expel me but to deny my credit for algebra that year, requiring me to take it over during summer school. I cannot emphasize how upset I was at myself—but being honest is what kept me at that school. I learned that doing things thoroughly and honestly is the best way, and that dishonest shortcuts won't get you too far. Academic integrity should be taken seriously. If you cheat, you defeat the purpose of learning and you lie to yourself. I learned the hard way, but I learned my lesson."

It often seems as if people mostly notice good grades and other academic prowess, athletic victories or achievements, attractiveness, or successes in music or the arts. Being a so-called good person isn't the kind of thing that very often wins awards, gets recognition, earns scholarships, or draws public praise. But somehow small kindnesses can keep everything in perspective. All the awards in the world won't feel quite right if you don't feel positive about yourself inside. Think for a moment about a person you know who is especially kind to you in small, unrecognized ways. What kind of effect does that person have on your life? If you have ever performed a small kindness, how did it make you feel, even if no one really seemed to thank you for it?

"One positive experience I had in high school was being treasurer of my school's Key Club, a high school community service group sponsored by Kiwanis International," says Michael Nahum, from Oceanside, New York, now in college. "I enjoyed helping out by doing different types of service—we did walkathons for the March of Dimes, Long Island AIDS Association, and others. They were fun, and I was helping people. Now, in college, this also influenced me to pledge the Alpha Phi Omega service fraternity."

Carrie Chapman of Saranac Lake, New York, learned to appreciate volunteering gradually. "I was stacking cans on the high shelf [at a local food pantry], my arms aching with each movement, when it hit me—the scent of body odor, mothballs, and alcohol combined to create one pungent stench. When I turned to face the next customer, I wished I could run for the door and forget about this place altogether. Somehow I managed to stay, and I looked directly at Ernie. Everyone knew Ernie, although most pretended they didn't. He lived in a run-down house without running water. He stuttered because of Parkinson's disease, and it was an eternity before he was able to say to me, 'P-p-peas p-p-please.' With tears in my eyes and my breakfast ready to return from my stomach, I finished packing the food and sent Ernie on his way.

"Volunteering there began as a negative experience, what with seeing so many people with so little to live on, but in the long run it proved to be positive. After the initial shock, I grew fond of many of the 'regulars' and felt good about being able to help them, even if it was in a small way. This experience has affected my life in that I now make community service part of my everyday routine. Right now, I take part in the university's community service work study program by helping the teachers of the preschool classes at a local youth center. It helps me put my life in perspective. The smaller pleasures of my life are much more valuable when I take the time to enjoy them rather than taking them for granted. While we must all fend for ourselves in today's world, we must also give back to the community as a whole, even if it is only a can of peas here and there."

There has been a campaign nationwide to perform "random acts of kindness," in reaction to the self-centered "me decade" that was the eighties. Try performing such an act sometime in the next month—something small, for someone you know or someone you don't know, something that probably won't get you any attention or reward. It might tell you something about what you value in life.

Write here what you plan to do:

Later, look back on it. How did you feel about it? Would you do something like it again?

_____

_____

_____

_____

Many high school students, through various experiences, find that they value life more highly than almost anything else. "I was an ambitious eleventh-grader who thought success was the true meaning of life—to get into the best college was the number one priority," says Syracuse freshman Donny Reyes. "As I piled up extracurricular points for my college application, I met an upperclassman at a student government meeting. He was outgoing and popular and had climbed to the top of the social ladder of success. He was elected senior class president and had the world at his fingertips. He had a passion about him and seemed to be destined for greatness in politics. Everyone knew him. He, too, though, was caught up in the college-equals-success-equals-life attitude.

"This same student was found dead one evening, alone in his house. Apparently, he had experienced some difficulty in finding a college; the papers reported it as an accident. As I sat in the church, I thought of how little all those college application points meant. There is nothing wrong with setting goals and giving your all to achieve them, as long as you keep things in perspective. In high school, everyone defines success as going to college, getting a job, and getting rich. But each individual should define his or her own success. One thing I now know is true is that nothing is more precious than life, nothing. I shoot for my goals with all my heart, but when things get rough, I know it's okay because I have my health and my family. I am thankful just to be alive."

"My hallmate was on the phone cursing at his parents one night and he threatened to kill himself," says Cyrus Massoumi, a student from Palm Beach, Florida. "We laughed, thinking he was just messing around, until later that night when suddenly paramedics were carrying him out on a white stretcher, his lips blue and his face white. He had swallowed sleeping pills, trying to kill himself because he had failed an important history paper and he could no longer handle the pressure his parents had put on him to get straight A's. His parents didn't listen to him when he explained that he was trying, and we his dormmates didn't really hear him when he threatened to take his own life. Because of him, I realized the preciousness of life. And I realized that the best way to help someone is to listen."

Take a moment to think about what you value and what your code of ethics might be.

What do I value most in my life right now? What people, things, activities, or ideas are most important to me, and why?

1. _____

_____

2. _____

_____

3. _____

_____

About my ethical system: What do I consider to be good or proper things to do, things to have, or ways to behave?

1. _____

_____

2. _____

_____

3. _____

_____

What things to do, things to have, or ways to behave do I consider bad or immoral?

1. _____

_____

2. _____

_____

3. _____

_____

Goal-setting

Successful goal-setting is at the heart of achieving. If you dedicate yourself to a dream and do what it takes to bring it to life, you can accomplish almost anything. Goals give you the plan and the building blocks with which to construct your destiny, and these goals come in all shapes and sizes. You may have a goal to accomplish today, a week- or month-long goal, or a lifelong one. You may have goals that come from your religious beliefs, your coach, your parents, your boss, or your own dreams.

GOAL, noun.
1. the line or place at which a race is ended; the mark
2. the end or final purpose; the end to which a design tends or which a person aims to reach or accomplish

Your life is important to the world and people around you. What do you want to make of it? Your goals are important no matter what their scope. Whether you want to own a dry-cleaning business or hit in the major leagues like Dave Winfield, defining your goals will put you on the road to where you want to be.

Envisioning Your Goals

The first step is to figure out exactly what your goals are. Some guidelines:

Relate your goals to your interests and talents. You have already identified your interests and talents. Which of them do you most want to pursue? Which of them might eventually become a career choice? Envision yourself happy—what are you doing?

Use your imagination and creativity in order to push your goals to the limit. Let yourself imagine the wildest things. It's easy to underestimate your own imaginative and creative powers by focusing too hard on standard, practical concerns like money and security. Achieving an unusual goal might also provide for your basic needs. Don't think you are crazy or stupid for wanting to achieve something that seems out of reach. Everyone starts at the bottom—but some make it all the way to the top, whatever their version of "top" may be.

Look to your role models. Take a good look at the people you admire. If they are approachable or you know them, you can even talk to them. Think about how they reached their goals, about the struggle they went through to achieve. If you find people who have done what you want to do and have reached places where you want to go, you can use their example to map out your way to similar goals.

Have some faith in your drive and your gut instincts. When you know in your heart that you truly love something, or that some idea constantly drives you, this may lead you to the goal you should be pursuing. Don't deny your deepest instincts. Just evaluate them realistically.

Joon Lee, a law student at George Washington University in Washington, D.C., set two goals as a student at Tottenville High School in Staten Island, New York. One stemmed from a deep-seated drive to overturn a stereotype, and the other came from his interest in politics. "As a Korean American, I was intent on doing all I could to overcome the racial stereotypes I got teased about. A lot of the kids I was in school with had this narrow, ignorant view of Korean Americans. They thought all we did was study and that we excelled only in math and science."

To buck the stereotypes, Joon pursued sports in high school and starred as an outside linebacker on his high school football team. He didn't even *like* his math and science classes. Instead, he set a second goal—to be involved in politics—and today is on his way to becoming a lawyer in Washington, D.C.

Shaun Crawford sets her goals by considering what's important to her as well as the examples set by her aunt and others around her. "My immediate goal is to finish high school with good grades and without getting into trouble. To do that, I attend class every day—and I am one of the few kids who actually do that. Plus, I am on the Key Club and junior prom committees."

Working toward Your Goals

Once you set your main goals, it can be hard to figure out where to start. The key is to use smaller goals as steps toward the larger ones. I put types of big and small goals into three related pairs: (1) practical and dream; (2) short-term and long-term; and (3) general and specific.

1. Practical Goals and Dream Goals

Practical goals will get you through the day; they are often the building blocks upon which we construct larger goals. They help you accomplish what is important to you on a daily basis. They might concern the amount of time you study, the amount of time you spend in front of the television, or the amount of exercise you get.

Practical goals might also lead you toward a dream goal, as they did in Jackie Spence's case. Jackie grew up in the second largest city in the Philippines. "Most of us in Cebu City were poor and didn't have the advantages that so many people take for granted in the United States. When I was in high school, my aunt wrote me letters from the United States, where she was living, telling me about the opportunities there to work hard and get ahead. It became my dream to live in the United States, and I knew that if I worked hard, learned English well, and wrote well, I might get there. I ended up winning a scholarship for my high school tuition and made it to the United States several years later. It would not have been possible without my determination to do better."

Dream goals are more far-reaching and speak to your imagination. In your wildest dreams, what is it you would most like to do, see, or become? Before you start imagining yourself as the latest lottery winner, remember two important considerations. First, dream goals can be as outlandish as you like so long as they have some connection to the interests and talents you mapped out for yourself. Second, you must be willing to commit yourself in some way to achieving your dream goal, however small the steps you take toward it.

These are the practical and dream goals of Maria Lopez, a high school junior in Albuquerque, New Mexico:

My Practical Goals Are

1. Spend at least twenty minutes a day reading the newspaper.
2. Never watch television before completing all my homework.
3. Try to get along better with my family.
4. Eat better, exercise, and stay away from drugs and alcohol.
5. Read at least one library book a month.

My Dream Goals Are

1. Be a doctor in the Peace Corps.
2. Open my own clothing boutique.

Fill in your own practical and dream goals below.

My Practical Goals Are

1. _____

2. _____

3. _____

4. _____

5. _____

My Dream Goals Are

1. _____

2. _____

2. Short-term Goals and Long-term Goals

You can also think of your goals in terms of time. Short-term goals are those that you aim to reach in six months or less. These goals may include the grades you hope to make next quarter or the date you hope to get for next week's dance. As you define your short-term goals, keep them consistent with your long-term goals. For example, if your short-term goal is to get good grades next quarter, your long-term goal might be to raise your GPA one point this year. Short-term goals help you achieve long-term goals by taking you through step by step, and long-term goals help you identify where to set up short-term goals.

Here are the long-term and short-term goals of Bryce Edwards, a high school senior in Portland, Oregon:

My Long-term Goals Are

1. Graduate from college.
2. Get the job I want most.
3. Get married and have a family.
4. Build a home in the country.

My (Corresponding) Short-term Goals Are

1. Study as hard as I can.
2. Find out what I can now about the college application process.
3. Think of ways to meet new friends and develop the friendships I have.
4. Discover career options that would allow me to live in the country.

List your own long-term and short-term goals below.

My Long-term Goals Are

1. _____

2. _____

3. _____

4. _____

My (Corresponding) Short-term Goals Are

1. _____

2. _____

3. _____

4. _____

3. General and Specific Goals

General goals focus your attention on the broad themes that can help you direct your life today and always. General goals might include doing your best or helping others. Specific goals flesh out how you will achieve general goals. You might have more specific goals than general goals, because it can take several specific goals to reach a general goal.

Carol Mylovsky, a high school senior in Harrisburg, Pennsylvania, writes:

My General and Specific Goals Are

1. My first general goal is to become more interested in learning. My specific goals are (1) concentrate in my classes, (2) read more books and newspapers to expand my horizons, and (3) pay attention to worthwhile television shows and movies.

2. My second general goal is to make a contribution to the world. My specific goals are (1) do volunteer work, and (2) get good grades so I can get a good job that will allow me to help others.

3. My third general goal is to have lots of friends. My specific goals are (1) be a good friend to others, (2) join clubs and activities that will allow me to meet new friends, (3) keep an open mind so I will be receptive to others, and (4) build my confidence.

4. My fourth general goal is to keep in good shape. My specific goals are (1) eat right, (2) try out for a team, and (3) take up jogging and aerobics.

Lay out your own general and specific goals.

My General and Specific Goals Are

1. My first general goal is _____

   _____

   My specific goals are _____

   _____

   _____

2. My second general goal is _____

   _____

   My specific goals are _____

   _____

   _____

3. My third general goal is _____

   _____

   My specific goals are _____

   _____

   _____

4. My fourth general goal is _____

   _____

   My specific goals are _____

   _____

   _____

Once you begin to work toward your goals, you will have a clearer idea of where the moves you make are taking you. Of course, everyone stumbles and loses sight of goals from time to time. You'll go a day, a week, or even a month and not accomplish what you wanted to do. You'll get frustrated sometimes. But even an athlete like Deion Sanders didn't take to baseball right away—he was released by the New York Yankees before signing with the Atlanta Braves and batting .533 in the World Series for them. Be willing to experiment with your routine in order to accomplish the goals you have set.

Jeannine Young learned about goal-setting on the soccer field in Cinnaminson, New Jersey. "During my four years as a member of the soccer team, each individual worked hard to accomplish her own goals, which in turn helped the team achieve team goals. As a team, we all had drive and were goal-oriented. We communicated when things didn't go well—if anyone was not pulling her weight, as a team we would confront that member and let her know how we felt. Through hard work, desire, and determination, we won the state championship three years during my high school career. Although at the time I looked upon that goal as far-fetched, we got there through our commitment. Nothing you want comes to you easily in a team environment. Now, when I encounter a teamwork project, I know that it won't be easy, but if everyone works together, the goal will be attained."

The key to working successfully toward your goals is to take everything one step at a time—maybe one *day* at a time, or one practical, short-term, or specific goal at a time. Each "building block" goal will carry you further toward your larger goals. I couldn't run my marathon until I could do one lap of the track . . . a two-mile run . . . a 10K run . . . and a ten-miler. It takes time to build up strength and knowledge, no matter what you want to achieve.

Reassessing and Modifying Your Goals

You face failure every time you try to accomplish anything—that's the risk you take. Evaluate your progress as you go by asking yourself questions like these: Am I getting anywhere? Do I still want or need the same goals? If you want to give up, make sure you haven't mistaken a need to change a goal for a desire to quit when the going gets rough. If you know you are seeking something you truly want, stick with it through the tough places and you will be rewarded for your hard work. Jeff Zimon, a graduate of Duxbury High School in Massachusetts, found that out. "My freshman year, all I cared about was basketball, and I would shoot hoops every day after school until the sun went down. At the tryouts in late November, I was confident that I would make the JV team. I gave my very best effort and thought my attitude was great. But when the team was posted, my name was not there.

"My immediate reaction was that my basketball career and my life were over! I cried all night. I overreacted by deciding never to play basketball again. But after a week my parents persuaded me to play for the freshman team. During the course of the year I gained confidence and dominated the freshman league, and when after four games the JV coach asked me if I wanted to play for him, my big smile answered his question! This incident taught me never to give up and not to overreact when I'm faced with setbacks. I have learned to be satisfied with the result if I know I have given one hundred percent effort."

But if you decide, maybe even with the advice of others, that you were mistaken in the goal you chose to pursue, you can certainly reassess that goal. Maybe you will decide to abandon it altogether. Or perhaps you only need to modify it.

REASSESS, verb.
  to reevaluate; to look at again to determine importance
MODIFY, verb.
  to change or alter

Look specifically at why you don't seem to be achieving your goal. Sometimes you just need to get psyched up again, but other times you need to make a change. Becky Amato had a rude awakening in her effort to get high grades in a schedule full of honors classes. "One day in geometry class, I got a test back with a very bad grade. I was so certain that I was going to fail geometry that I hyperventilated in front of the whole class. The teacher rushed me down to the nurse, and a counselor taught me breathing techniques so that I could handle the stress if it got to me again. I ended up realizing that I couldn't take an entire semester of honors classes!" Becky rethought her goal and changed a couple of classes.

Don't get too down on yourself if you don't achieve a goal. Sometimes you think you have a goal in hand and it eludes you at the last second—in such a case, it's important to give yourself a chance to reassess and look at alternatives. Sara Verhey had this kind of experience in Peoria, Illinois, as a member of the speech team at her high school. "My partner and I did a piece where I was a flamboyant teacher and he was a meek, careless student. We practiced for hours on end, and it paid off in regional and conference championships.

"Then we came to the sectional tournament, which would qualify us for state. I never felt more accomplished than I did when we heard the roar of applause at the end of our piece. I thought we had it in the bag. Then the master of ceremonies announced our names as the fourth-place team—only the top three qualified for state. I thought my one dream and accomplishment had been stolen from under my nose. I later discovered that a time violation of two and a half seconds dropped us from first to fourth place."

Sara learned that despite high hopes, expectations won't always be fulfilled, and sometimes you will have to go back to the drawing board and fix what went wrong. Then it's time to gear up and set your sights high again with the new knowledge you've gained.

Priorities

Each individual has a variety of things that interest him or her. Perhaps you've been to a concert recently and thought how great it would be to be able to play a guitar or sing a duet. Maybe you watched the Super Bowl last year and wondered what it would be like to throw a sixty-yard spiral for a touchdown. Maybe you've seen articles about relief workers helping the poor in a foreign country and thought that might be something you would enjoy doing someday. You know it takes time and commitment, but how do you decide what path you want to take?

It's not easy to sort through all your interests and decide what is most important to you. Some interests are passing, and some are worthy of commitment. Most of us simply have too many interests to get to. In all likelihood, you're just not going to have the chance to be a rock star, professional quarterback, and relief worker all at the same time.

If your family needs some extra money to get by, your school and work time might be your priorities. If you have a beautiful voice and want to become a singer, your priorities might be school, rehearsal, and voice lessons. If you are very close to your family, spending time with them will be a priority.

PRIORITY, noun.
  1. that which is first in order, time, or importance
  2. that which converts an interest into a commitment
PRIORITIZE, verb.
  1. to arrange according to priority

For those of you who already have an idea of what interests you most, you might want to just home in on that one interest and commit yourself completely to it. Sometimes that's necessary to get you where you want to go. When Connie McGuire was at Northwood High, in Silver Spring, Maryland, she prioritized her obligations in order to achieve her dream: a chance to train with the American Ballet Theatre in New York City. Her only two priorities were ballet (first) and school (a close second). A guidance counselor told her she could accommodate her ballet practice by arranging for a special class schedule. So from 8 to 11:30 a.m. Connie attended academic classes, and from 12 noon to 6:00 p.m. she took ballet classes. Weekends meant five more hours of ballet and a part-time job to help pay her way.

Despite her grueling schedule, Connie finished high school in three years and realized her goal of dancing in New York at the age of seventeen. Says Connie, "In ballet, as in gymnastics, you have to go for it when you're young, and go all out, if you're going to do it at all. For me, it was a case of prioritizing my goals and doing what I had to do. I'll always have that to look back on and feel proud of. While my dance career in New York lasted only a year, it was a dream come true."

You can miss out on some opportunities, though, if you pursue a single goal to the exclusion of everything else. Other interests can provide benefits that help in ways you haven't thought about. Jim Lindsey passes on some advice from experience: "I think that overemphasizing academics is a bad thing. In school I was engrossed in academics, and I wasn't completely fulfilled. Now I'm interested in all sorts of things, taking care of my body, reading, being with my friends, going places. I'm more well rounded, and consequently a more fulfilled person."

WELL-ROUNDED, adjective.
  the state of being in balance, especially in terms of interests and activities

When I was in high school, the more active I was, the better I did in my studies. When I was a freshman, I had nothing going on in my life outside school except baby-sitting and sewing. There wasn't much happening, so I didn't really have to prioritize. My study time just expanded to fit the available after-school time, and I lacked focus because I had a lot of time on my hands. Then in my sophomore and junior years I was a bit busier. I began to learn to juggle everything that I wanted to do. I did best in school my senior year when I was working at the restaurant, volunteering at a hospice, and maintaining my position as president of the senior class.

Thinking through your priorities can also help you discover why you aren't doing so well in a particular area. For those of you who are not performing as well in school right now as you would like, try to analyze why that is. Are you devoting too much time to team sports, or to a part-time job? Your activities and work are valuable, but you might have to scale back a little for the sake of your education. Think creatively about your time and shift an hour or so a day over to homework time. Devoting all your time to outside pursuits can be just as limiting as concentrating only on your studies. Maintain your balance.

Very seldom do people have *everything* they want. When you put one priority above another, you make a trade-off—a decision about what you want most and what you can do without.

TRADE-OFF, noun.
   a choice involving the exchange of one or more benefits for others
   deemed more desirable

Nicole Caplan had to face that kind of decision as a high school student in Guttenberg, New Jersey. "In 1992 my mother decided to leave her job. Starting her own business was not easy, and she really needed help. At this point I was heavily involved in high school, especially sports, and I was chosen to captain my basketball team, which consumed most of my spare time. I had to choose between what was extremely important to me and what would help my mom get her business on track. I knew that if I quit basketball I would have no chance of being captain again or winning scholarships. But there was a chance that my mom's business might fall through, and after some contemplation, I realized that her business was just as much for us as it was for her. I chose to help my mom. This experience taught me how to prioritize and make important decisions. Sometimes life requires certain sacrifices for a higher cause, and you have to weigh the options and figure out what has the most priority."

As important and rewarding as it is to be well rounded and to involve yourself in a variety of activities, that, too, can go too far. If you spread yourself too thin, you may get to the point where you aren't getting much out of anything. In that case, your teachers/coaches/parents/ bosses may not be getting much out of *you*! Being well rounded isn't just a matter of keeping a lot of things going. You have to know what takes priority, and you have to change when priorities change. Sometimes you will need to discard activities when things go overboard; you will have to quit what you feel is least useful to you.

Sarah Lyman Kravits had to force herself to learn how to scale back her activities more than a few times in high school. "I always thought I could do it all, and then I would find out the consequences only after I had tried it and gotten exhausted or even sick. My father used to force me to take rest days off school every once in a while. Bit by bit, with his help, I began to say no to a few things—I didn't take the Saturday math course that so many of my friends took, I reduced my dance class load during field hockey season, and I turned down positions of responsibility in clubs. That was the only way I could get my work done and still be somewhat sane."

Juggling Your Priorities: Time Management

Once you establish your goals, prioritize them, and make your trade-offs, you need to manage the twenty-four hours you have each day in order to do what you want to do. If you can successfully juggle your priorities, you will get more out of your time. Right now you can begin by working with a day or week at a time. As time goes on, you'll apply this same technique to longer stretches of time, like a month, six months, and even a year—you'll engage in "long-term planning," or, as it's called in business, "strategic planning." It means looking ahead and planning for what's important to you.

You can manage your time in three simple steps:

1. Think through what you have to accomplish in a day (or week, month, etc.).
2. Map out a course that allots time for each task.
3. Do it. (The most important step!)

Here's a sample schedule—one of mine from my sophomore year of high school.

8:00	Carpool		
9:00–3:00	School		
3:00–5:00	Car wash for ski club fund-raising		
6:00–10:30	Baby-sit at Brewers'		
	Studying:	6–7	One chapter (12) biology
		7–8	Begin *Lord of the Flies* paper
		8–9	Read chapter 8 history
		9–9:30	Review Spanish for quiz
		9:30–10:30	TV or phone or play

Some parts of this day were obligatory, such as school and the ski club fund-raising event. The secret to the time management of this day was the study time while I baby-sat. Fortunately, it was a six-month-old baby. If it had been an older child, I would have been studying until midnight because I would have been playing with him until eight-thirty or nine. Either that, or I wouldn't have studied at all, and it would have hurt me in my classes the next day.

Start by dividing your everyday life into these four categories of activity. *School, Extracurriculars/Fun, Work,* and *Family/Friends.* No one person can be equally committed and successful in all four of these areas. But devoting time to each, in some (if unequal) amounts, is important to being well rounded. This is your chance to take a look at your life, see how you feel about how it's going, and change your priorities if you feel the need. People change all the time, and needs and priorities change accordingly.

1. What classes are my priorities at school?

_____

_____

_____

How much time per day do I spend at school? _____

_____

How much time on homework? _____

_____

2. With what activities am I involved? How much time do they take?

   School-related: _____

   _____

   Non-school-related: _____

   _____

3. If I have any job or jobs, where do I work?

   _____

   _____

   How much time do I work each week?_____

   _____

4. Do I spend time regularly with family or friends? Who are they?

   _____

   _____

   How much time do I spend each week with them (this may be hard

   to figure out—just estimate)?_____

   _____

Before you begin to schedule your time, look at this map of your life and decide if you need to redistribute your energy. For example, if you are big into your friends and your job—maybe all of your best friends are *at* your job—then you might want to focus harder on school and activities. Or if you exhaust yourself studying and going to hours of soccer practice, consider spending more time to get to know people around you.

Now you can make your own schedules. First, do a specific one for a day this week; put stars in the priority column for activities or events that should take priority.

TIME	ACTIVITY	PRIORITY?
7:00 a.m.		
8:00 a.m.		
9:00 a.m.		
10:00 a.m.		
11:00 a.m.		
12:00 noon		
1:00 p.m.		
2:00 p.m.		
3:00 p.m.		
4:00 p.m.		
5:00 p.m.		
6:00 p.m.		
7:00 p.m.		
8:00 p.m.		
9.00 p.m.		
10:00 p.m.		

Take a look at the week as a whole. You don't have to list all your activities—just use the schedule to get a sense of the most important priorities during the week.

SUNDAY	MONDAY	TUESDAY	WEDNESDAY	THURSDAY	FRIDAY	SATURDAY

Making schedules like this isn't for everyone. Even those who like to schedule all their time will forget to do it sometimes. But scheduling is worth a try—it can really help you manage your time. Joanne Ebeling discovered the value of scheduling while pursuing her favorite sport. "Basketball taught me time management, because during high school I had to fit in working and homework with basketball practices and games. I could not waste days. I had to make sure I used my time productively. This skill really helps me in college—time is plentiful if it is scheduled the right way. I am so glad I stuck with basketball!"

Katy O'Connor also had to schedule her time: "Cheerleading taught me how to budget my time efficiently. Practices lasted two or more hours after school. I also had obligations to other extracurricular activities after school, and then after practice I had to do my homework. There was no time to relax—cheerleading kept me organized and did not leave time for procrastination. Now that I am in college, being without cheerleading is one of the adjustments I have had to make. I need to become involved to keep myself organized and prioritized. I have started to work on my goal—I joined a business club and am taking an aquacize course. I realize more and more what cheerleading gave to me."

Even if you think scheduling yourself will be annoying, give it a test run for one week and see if it helps you stay organized and on top of things. It is an important step in the process you can follow to achieve what you want in life—you define your values, set and prioritize your goals, and finally organize your time so that you can work toward your goals in the best way possible.

▪ 6 ▪

BECOMING MOTIVATED
What You'll Need to Move Ahead

I looked forward to studying fascinating subjects taught by people who understood what they were talking about. I imagined meeting brilliant students who would challenge me to stretch my mind and work instead of going skating . . . [I imagined myself] with my lessons done well enough so that I led the classmates who hated what they were studying.

MARGARET MEAD
Anthropologist
1901–1978

From the small town of New Hope, Pennsylvania, where she lived in 1918, it looked as though seventeen-year-old Margaret Mead's dream of going to college (a still-uncommon career path for a young woman of her time) wouldn't come true. Her father's business ventures had recently failed, and money was scarce; therefore her parents wanted Margaret to work. They had a friend come to their home and talk to Margaret about working in New Hope as a medical assistant. While she understood the circumstances her parents were in, she had motivated herself to reach for the sky—to achieve all she knew she was capable of achieving. The idea of lowering her sights made her unhappy.

Her parents picked up on Margaret's cue—her ambition and confidence convinced them that she had to go to college. They decided first that she would attend her father's alma mater, DePauw, which wasn't as expensive as other schools they had considered such as Bryn Mawr or Wellesley. After a year, unhappy with the odd chemistry of coeducation and with not fitting into the social scene, Margaret persuaded her father to let her apply to the all-women's Barnard College, in New York. There her motivation paid off, as she used her energy, imagination, and willingness to explore to pursue what was then a new field of science: cultural anthropology, the study of human nature as influenced by different cultures and societies. After graduation, Margaret's fieldwork in such distant outposts as Samoa and elsewhere in the South Pacific won her fame and respect around the world. She became a major author read by anthropology students everywhere and an accomplished public speaker on the lecture circuit. She published her final major work when she was seventy-six years old, not long before her death.

When I look at what successful people like Margaret Mead have accomplished, I almost always see a combination of certain qualities. She started out with a positive *attitude* about her abilities; she took the *initiative* necessary to put everything in motion; she made a *decision* about what her highest-priority goals were; she *motivated* herself to pursue her dreams; and she stayed *committed* to her goals until she reached them. This particular path to success takes a huge amount of energy and strength, but it leads to the top more surely than any other.

Attitude

How do you view your life, your friends, your school, and the world? Is everything great, or does life consist of one problem after another?

ATTITUDE, noun.
1. the manner of acting, feeling, or thinking that shows one's disposition
2. the posture or position of a person showing that person's mental state

---

Attitude colors everything you do. Bad or good, an attitude will affect how you feel about any experience as well as how others feel about you. Think about your "good days" and "bad days." On a really good day, not much will bother you. You're on a roll. Everything seems to go your way. Heather Bliss's attitude carried her through an important day. "This was the last stepping-stone to my ultimate soccer goal—we were playing a championship game in Syracuse's Carrier Dome. I sat on the sidelines hoping I'd be given the chance to play, and I was. As I walked onto the field, chills ran through my body. I played the best game of my life that day. I focused entirely on the game, never noticing the layers of blood that encompassed my knees or my friends cheering and yelling my name. I realized that striving for goals is worth all the hard work I put into it. My positive attitude led me to feel the ultimate satisfaction that day, even though when the game ended, we had lost 2 to 1."

Then there are the bad times, when nothing can go right. Everything either bores you or troubles you. It can be really hard to maintain a good attitude in high school. Pressure to get good grades, hang out with the "right" crowd, and keep up with the latest stylish look can combine with other negatives like problems at home or relationship headaches. If you go through a period where nothing seems to go your way, it's hard to convince yourself that anything ever will. "My first two years in high school were hard because I didn't know anyone and just didn't like the school," says Tiffany Moncrieffe, a recent graduate of Central Park Secondary School in New York City. "My attitude wasn't to my advantage. I found myself getting into trouble with students and teachers—I was in the principal's office all the time. At parent conferences, teachers spoke highly of my work, but then they would say my bad attitude was stopping me from moving ahead. My parents would talk to me, but it went in one ear and out the other. I just didn't care."

Your overall attitude can make the difference between success and failure. I had a bad attitude for more than half of high school because I resented always being compared to my brothers. From the moment I entered high school, my teachers perked up when they figured out I was a member of the "Carter family," and continually asked about what my brothers were doing, talking about how wonderful they were. Their accomplishments hung like a cloud over me because I wanted my own identity; I wanted to be liked on my own merits. In reaction to everything they stood for, I rebelled. I pursued activities different from everything that they did—if they worked on the newspaper, I worked on the yearbook, and if they participated in debates, I joined the student council. I also didn't bother to apply myself in class as they had done.

Only later in school, when I began to appreciate my own unique abilities, did I appreciate the accomplishments of my brothers. Only by forging my own way, as full of wrong turns as it was, could I grow to accept who I was and realize that I was just as intelligent as they were, even though I had been an underachiever. After I got that dose of reality and self-esteem, I was able to turn my attitude around and benefit from it without being threatened by my brothers.

Tiffany got turned around after a while as well. "At the end of the freshman year, I was sure I would get an academic award, since I had done so well in my work, but I didn't receive any. I wanted to get back at everyone because of that. Then one day one of my teachers spoke with me—I acted like I wasn't listening, but I was. She said I wasn't hurting anyone but myself, and that my actions weren't getting me anywhere. It hit me that it was true. I watched my cousins graduate and go off to college to try to make something of themselves, and I wanted to do the same. I knew I couldn't keep up this attitude if I wanted to get somewhere in life. Day by day, I continued to grow up. Instead of arguing with teachers, I was holding conversations with them. They, my parents, and my classmates continued to help me improve my attitude. The award that really turned me around was the Who's Who among American High School Students award, which I received for two consecutive years. That showed me I was recognized for my attitude in a positive way. I graduated high school and am now majoring in business management in college. If I hadn't made the change in my attitude, I wouldn't be where I am now."

When you do manage to have a positive attitude about yourself and your abilities, it can really propel you forward, as it finally did for me in my senior year. How can you develop—and, more important, maintain—a positive attitude? One way is to take everything as it comes and not accept defeat. Disappointments and setbacks happen to everybody, even though you think you're the only one with problems. People who say they've never stumbled are lying. If you know that tough times come along every once in a while, you'll be able to take them in stride and get back on your feet faster.

Try to find the good in any situation. Ask yourself what you can learn from the experience, what you can enjoy about it, or how it can benefit you. You can't change the fact that good and bad things will continue to happen, but you have the power to adjust your perspective. Kristina Hahn was able to do just that as a member of her school's track relay team in Saddle Brook, New Jersey. "I found it especially hard when I would run a fantastic race, hand off the baton, and watch us lose because someone else seemed to slack off. I often walked off the track angry at my teammates. Although I didn't realize it then, they were doing the best they could. I learned from experience that getting mad and holding a grudge over something completely out of my control just makes things worse. We all have to work together despite our faults. My job is to work up to my own potential and never settle for second best."

Here's how Raquel Ramirez, a student from Dallas, Texas, describes herself:

1. I have a good attitude about
   (1) playing team sports, (2) being with my friends, and
   (3) my science and math classes.

2. I have a bad attitude about
(1) not being allowed to dress the way I want to and (2) doing my homework.

Talk about your own attitudes here:

1. I have a good attitude about

_____

_____

2. I have a bad attitude about

_____

_____

3. I will have a better attitude if

_____

_____

Initiative

INITIATIVE, noun.
1. the action of taking the first step
2. the characteristic of being able to originate new ideas or methods; enterprise

Initiative spurs you to follow through on an important decision. It's that curiosity and ingenuity inside you that is constantly thinking of new and improved ways of seeing and doing things. Initiative is what helps you take a step when no one else around you is encouraging you to do so.

Developing initiative can help you in a couple of ways. You won't always be able to reach the goals you set for yourself. That's normal.

When it happens, however, you need to be able to keep moving by taking up an alternative or revised plan. Going back to the drawing board that way takes initiative—and it shows a willingness to take action, responsibility, and control. A sudden event gave Wexford, Pennsylvania, native Kelly Hines a chance to learn about her own initiative. "My team was only thirteen seconds away from a victory against our rival, and as I dribbled down the court, I suddenly felt an immense blow to my body. I was carried off on a stretcher, and after a week's stay in the hospital, I was diagnosed with severe damage to my spinal cord and neck, affecting my vision, sensation, and motion. To play basketball again was forbidden. Hearing that meant the loss of my dream and my scholarship to play Division I basketball at Colgate University.

"Devastated at first, I soon realized that I had to be a role model to my team and show courage, leadership, and a positive attitude. I took the initiative to attend every practice and game. Right now I am confused because I don't know what my next long-term goal will be. But I am at peace because I feel that everything happens for a purpose. I am now concentrating on other activities that I enjoy, to develop new strengths. I have come to realize that basketball taught me teamwork, dedication, commitment, patience, tenacity, sharing, working toward goals, and most important, realizing that the calls are not always going to go the way you want them to."

Initiative is also important because you are emerging as an independent person responsible for your own life and actions. You won't always be in an environment like school or home where you have parents, teachers, administrators, and other caretakers telling you what to do and how and when to do it. Bit by bit now, and more later, you will need to be the one setting the goals and deciding on the steps to take to pursue them, or you might end up being unable to separate yourself from your couch and remote control, and it could be hard to find someone who will pay your rent!

Many of the stories you've already heard from students and former students show how they took initiative. When James Morris broke up a fight between two girls and their boyfriends, his individual initiative led him to step into a dangerous situation when no one encouraged him—in fact, people probably would have stopped him had they known what he wanted to do. Since Deena Mottola didn't find the kind of activity she wanted already established at the school, she took the intiative to start a Teen Crisis Hot Line in her school library.

Kirk Jennings shows a strong sense of initiative in his studies. "I like to challenge myself and I like to compete. I think it is important to pick up any kind of literature and read it, because you may learn something that can help you." Taking the initiative to read material beyond what you are assigned in your classes will give you an extra wealth of knowledge and experience. You are taking initiative right now by reading this book! Holmes Osborne, now a college student at Syracuse University, had an experience that gave him a new outlook similar to Kirk's. "When I took French in high school, I had never before studied a foreign language. I had problems—but I was not the only one; half the class was in the same situation. I would go early in the morning before school every day and study in the French room to improve my test scores.

"Then the teacher offered one hundred points to any student who read a particular novel. I had never read a book of this length before, but I decided to do it. The points I got for reading it were enough to earn me an A in the course. The funny thing was, I was the only student who took advantage of the offer! I didn't understand why other students didn't try to earn the extra points. I felt that the entire class was lazy because of this. From then on, in class I associated with the hard workers. Since most of my friends took the easy way in school, I stayed away from them while in class. My grade point average sharply increased. I realized that classes are for learning and not for socializing. Today, when my friends compare how many classes they have skipped and ask me, I say 'none.' "

Decision-making

Making important decisions about your life, and knowing how to follow through, can be agonizing and difficult. But certain strategies can make this integral part of life more manageable.

DECISION-MAKING, noun.
  1. The act of making up one's mind
  2. The reaching or giving of a judgment or conclusion

You can apply a positive attitude and a willingness to take initiatives to the many decisions that you make as a high school student. The consequences of some decisions, such as whether to stay in school or whether to use birth control, can affect you for the rest of your life. Other decisions are not so earth-shattering but still matter to you.

Choices are often less than clear, particularly right now when you're facing so many issues all at once. What classes should you take? What friendships or relationships are worth your time? How should you react when someone does you wrong? How hard should you work? Should you tune out your family or make an effort to communicate? What is your future, and whom should you turn to for advice? These are just the tip of the iceberg. You make decisions every day, and they can confuse and trouble you.

Some of you have some serious disadvantages to deal with, and it may be extremely difficult for you to cope with all the pressures facing you right now. If you focus on what lies within your power to change, you can come up with a plan that will take you in the best direction possible. We all have factors in our lives that are out of our control. The key to finding where your decision-making power lies is to focus on what you *can* control and to make the changes that you need. That's all that anyone can ask of you—or that you can ask of yourself.

When Tamika Leslie had a problem with the father of her son, she knew she could change neither his attitude and lifestyle nor the fact that he had fathered the child. But because she has custody, she realized she *could* control whom the child spends time with—and whom she spends time with herself. "I made a big decision when I left my son's father. I used to think that my son should have a life with both his parents together no matter what. But when I saw the danger my son's father was putting us in, I had to leave him and start a new safe life."

Taking the time to work your way through a decision can make it easier. I've found that this series of steps works best for me:

- *Name all the options.* What are all the ways your decision could go?
- *Think over the consequences of each option.* What do you think would happen each way? This is a good stage to ask for advice if you want to.
- *Choose the best option.* Consider the advice of others, but be the master of the final decision.
- *Carry it out.* Set everything in motion and sit tight for the ride.
- *Evaluate how things went.* Look at the situation after the fact and see if you think you made the correct decision or not, and why. You can learn from your choice, whether it turned out to be right or wrong.

Name all the options. There are at least two options, if not many more, to consider for every decision. Even if your only choices are to do something or not to do it, that's two right there. Sometimes there might be an in-between option, as in deciding whether to cut your hair short, leave it long, or just get a trim. Give yourself a little time—sometimes all the options don't surface at once. Maybe if the homecoming dance is coming up, you think your choices are to ask a date to go or not to go at all. But some more ideas might pop up. You could get a group of single friends together and go as a group, you could wait to be asked by someone, or you might just go on your own and see what happens.

Think over the consequences of each option. With each option come consequences—circumstances that would follow the choice if you made it. When you are ready to make a decision, you are at a crossroads. The options from which you have to pick are the paths that lead away from where you are, and the consequences are the results and events that lie a little ways down the paths.

CONSEQUENCE, noun.
   a result of an action or process; an outcome; an effect

Take Jim Lindsey's decision about what classes to take. "Academics were very stressful," he says. "I was a perfectionist, and I would spend hours making sure my work was fault-free. I think I rebelled against the pressure by making a decision not to go for the honors classes. I backed away and didn't even try to get in because it was too much pressure. I would have driven myself crazy in the more rigorous classes. I felt like I knew myself and did as much as I could handle. I did pretty well anyway and got into Cornell."

Jim looked at the potential consequences of each option. The consequences of the first option, knocking himself out to get into the honors classes, were:

- He would have to work hard constantly to keep up in the higher-level classes.
- His perfectionism would lead him to overload himself with work.
- His work would probably earn him good grades, which would help him get into college.

The consequences of deciding to stick with the regular classes were:

- He wouldn't have to work quite so hard to keep up.
- His perfectionism would lead him to try as hard as he could with the work he had to do.
- Working hard would earn him good grades in these classes as well.

It was easier for Jim to make the decision after he had looked at the consequences of each option—the second set of consequences appealed much more to him.

Who do you feel makes most of your decisions? Is it you, or someone else, or do they just seem to happen on their own? Who's in charge? Before you make your decision, consult other people if you feel you want advice or a different perspective. I think the best situation is when you take advantage of advice from knowledgeable people but make final decisions on your own. When it comes down to it, it's your life, and you have to live with the consequences. If you make all of your decisions completely on your own, you may be putting a bit too much pressure on yourself; also, missing out on advice from more experienced people might cost you some time and energy if you make problematic decisions.

"I quit the varsity basketball team my senior year," says New York City native Chet Bloom, now a college student. "I never got along with the coach, which could have been my fault, but everyone who knew the man seemed to hate him. I played for him for three years and he never gave me a chance to show what I could do. When I played, I did well, and although I was not a star, I contributed to the team's development. My senior year I felt convinced that he thought I wasn't worthy of his attention, so I quit in the middle of the season. My parents hated the fact that I quit the team and advised me to continue, but I didn't. When they asked me if I missed playing, I would lie to them and say no, even though I really did. I will always regret that I quit the team and gave in to my fear and hatred for that man—I did what I felt he was forcing me to do. If I could do it again, I would stick with it and show him that I am a good player."

On the other hand, if you let everyone make decisions for you, you may lose control of your day-to-day life. Your best interests may not be served when you have no involvement in the decision, because as much as other people care about you, you know the most about your own needs. You are your own best friend. If you can limit your decision-making help to advice, new perspectives, or help on things you may have overlooked, you will find value in it.

By thinking through options with the input of her parents, Sarah Lyman Kravits made an important decision about her class schedule in her junior year. "I didn't know how to fill my elective. My father, who spent a year in Germany in college, thought I should take German. My mother felt I should learn how to type. They were at odds about it, so I had to do my own thinking about the consequences of each. German seemed fun and interesting, and I would be able to speak the language if I ever visited my father's old roommates in Munich. But if I took typing, I could develop good typing skills that, friends already in college had told me, would save me hours of time when writing my English papers. Plus, I knew that computers were popping up in all kinds of industries and that typing skills are essential to computer proficiency. So I took typing, and as a writer, I'm really glad I did. Dad still teaches me some German himself!"

Choose the best option. Now it's time to decide which option fits your needs and your life best. Go with your instincts. Almost all options will have some good points and some not-so-good or annoying aspects; just find the one with the most positive points and the fewest negative ones. There are rarely any perfect options, only best ones.

Carry it out. Action time! Do what you have decided to do, as soon as you possibly can. Try to avoid procrastination—decision-making enemy number one. We all have those times when we think to ourselves, "Maybe I'll do it later this afternoon . . . maybe I'll do it tomorrow . . . maybe I'll think about making a decision about that next week . . . or when everything in my life calms down!" Procrastination is one of the most common human traits.

PROCRASTINATION, noun.
　　the act of putting off an action or decision, often a painful or burdensome one, until a later date (can become a habit)

So often it seems that the easiest and most painless way to handle a situation is to ignore it in the hope that it will go away. This can cause any number of problems. My worst case of procrastination centered on studying at home my freshman year. I could find any excuse to put off doing my homework. I would talk on the phone, putter around the house, watch the news, or listen to the radio until around 9:00 p.m., when I would finally buckle down. Of course, by that time I was exhausted and tried in vain to compress a few hours' worth of studying into one hour before I fell asleep. I wasn't putting anything into my work, and my lackluster grades really showed it. The next year, I learned to face my procrastination head-on. I came right home from school, studied for an hour and a half before dinner, and then did a couple of hours after. That way I still had time for my other fun stuff and I didn't feel guilty that I hadn't done any work. If I had plans in the evening I would compress all my studying into the after-school study time and skip dinner.

"In high school I often procrastinated with my work," says Joshua Weissman of Searingtown, New York. "I felt that I worked well under pressure. But during one assignment, my method backfired. I had waited too long to start and I was in for a lot of trouble, because seniors needed to complete this particular assignment to graduate. My teacher gave us six weeks to find and research a topic. Instead of using that time constructively, I waited until the last week, and then I had to pick a topic I had no interest in. The lack of research time left me with voids in my research and analysis, and the fact that I wasn't interested in the subject made the work seem much more difficult and tedious. I got the paper done, but the lack of preparation resulted in flaws that I could have prevented."

When you know that you need to take action, do yourself a favor by acting as soon as possible. This doesn't mean that you should make a move before you have thought it out thoroughly. Take the time you need to consider all options and to examine why you feel a change is necessary. Ask for advice and sort things through. But move as soon as you are ready. The longer you procrastinate, the more of *your own time* you waste!

When I was sixteen, the summer before my senior year of high school, my oldest brother, David, wanted me to spend the summer studying in Guatemala. At first I was open to the suggestion, but the more I thought about it and the closer it came to summer, the more it scared me. My instincts said, "Don't go." On the purely practical side, I didn't even know how to speak Spanish and I had never spent time away from home except for one week of summer camp. This was one of the most difficult decisions I had to make. Although I wanted to go to another country and learn the language, this seemed like too big a step for me to take at that time. The worst part was that I procrastinated so long in telling my brother that he had already made all the arrangements for me. He was so angry with me that we didn't speak for six months. Still, I held my ground; it was my decision to make, and I had to live with the consequences.

The next year, I decided to spend the summer with a friend from Phoenix, studying and living with a family in Guadalajara, Mexico. I had a year to prepare myself for the trip, so by the time I went, I was pretty confident about it, although it was still a big decision for me, since it would be my first time away from home and family in a foreign country. The summer was filled with adventure. I took eight units of college-credit Spanish and learned both the language and the culture of Mexico, but that wasn't all—we wound up living with a divorced Mexican housewife whose children stole money from us, and we had to change homes halfway through the summer. There wasn't one dull moment in the entire trip, and we learned a lot about survival.

The experience with my brother had a twofold effect on my long-term decision-making. First, he taught me that I should keep the value of foreign study in mind when charting the course of my life. Second, I discovered that procrastination can cause more pain than just getting the decision over with. If I had told my brother when my doubts first appeared, I could have saved him the time and trouble he took to make the arrangements, and I could have saved us both the pain we felt during the six months we didn't talk. That was a rough period, but as a result, the lesson about procrastination definitely stuck with me.

Fear of the unknown often leads to procrastination. People like to stick with what is comfortable, sometimes even if it is not desirable. When you're not sure if making a decision will bring you greater happiness, you may hesitate. For better or for worse, the only way to know what is not yet known is to dive in! Eileen Cook took the plunge and was glad. "I changed my outlook by trial and error. I took stands slowly at first, in classes or lunchtime discussions, and when I gained confidence in my own voice, I found it was much more comfortable. The nice thing about following your own lead is you can blaze trails that others will say are impassable. Now I have traveled through Europe extensively and started my own business where I do consulting for international rehabilitation organizations. If I hadn't taken a stand, I would be stuck in an entry-level job, living for my two-week vacation."

Evaluate how things went. Somehow this step often gets overlooked, because life is busy and you will find yourself moving right from one decision to the next. But the evaluation is important because that's where you look at what you have learned from the decision.

Melissa Romero, a high school student in Tucson, Arizona, made a decision that she later felt was wrong; however, somehow it helped her anyway. "My sophomore year, I thought I would do as well as my freshman year. It didn't turn out that way. We had open campus for lunch, and sometimes my friends and I wouldn't come back. Our second semester, a month before school ended, seven of us dropped out. My mother didn't know. I would get dropped off and leave campus before school started. Notices were sent home, and parents were finding out slowly but surely. Finally my best friend, Diana, told her parents about me because she didn't want to see me throw away my opportunities. That same day I had a long talk with my mom and told her. She wished I hadn't lied and had just told her if I didn't want to go to school. She was upset. But the experience with this bad decision led to my good decision to come back to school."

Motivation

MOTIVATION, noun.
  1. the inner drive that causes a person to do something or act in a certain way
  2. that which impels us to achieve our goals

Margaret Mead didn't know until graduate school that her interest was anthropology. What she did discover early on was that she felt motivated to explore and experience life to its fullest. You can make the same discovery. More important than knowing exactly where your life is going is having the motivation that will get you there.

Shaun Crawford gets inspiration from her aunt. "She shows me I can motivate myself to do anything. I don't have to depend on anyone to get what I want—I have confidence because of what she's taught me. I know I have a problem at times with my temper and a bad attitude, but I'm working on it. This year I got a job waitressing as suite runner in the sky boxes at the United Center, the new stadium where the Chicago Bulls play. I even got to meet Michael Jordan!"

What does it take to get motivated? It's not always easy. It's kind of a matter of getting in shape mentally—building "muscles" so that you have the power to get done what needs to be done. It might seem to you that motivation is a genetic trait of sorts—some people seem to have it and others just don't. Maybe you don't feel you are one of the motivated types, and you accept the "unmotivated" label as your own. That might not necessarily be true! You might be the kind of person who is motiated only to pursue your ultimate favorite subjects or activities. Garth Kravits fits that profile perfectly. "When I was in high school, I would get passes to leave other classes so that I could go work on things in the theater. I found I could only get motivated in my other classes if I could relate them back to theater, such as English when we read Shakespeare or history when we studied periods that helped me with a particular play. Unfortunately, if anything else was going on, I had no motivation at all to think about it or to work on it."

If you almost never feel motivated, think about any of your prior accomplishments. It doesn't matter how big or small they may have been, or whether they were even recognized by anyone other than yourself. It could be anything—beating your best time on the track, acing a test in a class you didn't take to so well at first, asking someone out that you had liked for a long time, scoring a hat trick for your soccer team, winning a position on the newspaper staff—no matter what, something motivated you to get yourself to the point where you could achieve your goal. If you want something badly enough, motivation will usually follow.

It's when you don't particularly want something that it's hard to get motivated. No one gets to do everything he or she likes in high school, and most people have to do a lot of things they wouldn't necessarily choose to do. At those times, try to discover other reasons why what you don't feel motivated to do might be a good idea anyway. Will it make your parents happy? Will it move you to the next level in a class? Will it help someone else?

Cynthia Nordberg discovered hidden values in something she had little motivation to do on her own. "I became nominally involved in a religious organization, and the study leader kept hassling me about doing more. I felt too busy with my classwork, but finally I gave in to her relentless prodding and went to a weekend retreat sponsored by the group. I wanted to get her off my back and figured that maybe if I went to this one event she wouldn't bother me for a while. I had a blast! I became more involved, and it was one of my richest experiences—I'm still enjoying the friendships I made then."

Lack of self-esteem also hinders motivation. You may have said things like these to yourself: I can't do it. I'm not smart enough. I'm not rich enough. I'm not attractive enough. I'm not coordinated or strong enough. I don't have enough time. I live in the wrong neighborhood. Nobody would want me anyway. These attitudes make you feel there's no point in even trying. If you can turn your attitude around and think positively about yourself, you will find it easier to get motivated. Sarah Czeladnicki, a graduate of Northport High School in New York State, motivated herself to work toward an important goal. "When I was in ninth grade, I decided to try out for the Tigerettes, the dance/kick line that was known for its great performances and also for the sisterhood that developed among the group. I had two disadvantages to overcome:

one, I had no previous dance instruction, and two, out of 130 girls, they were only taking 21. But I was determined to make it.

"When tryout time came, I had a Tigerette teach me the kicks so that I wouldn't have to worry about learning them at the actual tryout. I worked so hard during the first of the three practice days that my legs were in immense pain. I couldn't fall asleep at night because I kept repeating the routine over and over in my head. I stood next to the coach during practices so that she could see how hard I was working, I pulled my Achilles tendon from working so hard, but when auditions came around, I was ready. My kicks were high, I was precise with my moves, and I smiled from ear to ear. I made the first callback, and my second audition was even better. When I found out I made the line, it was one of the happiest moments of my life."

Somehow, many of life's greatest rewards are hidden until you motivate yourself to take action. When you challenge yourself to move forward and to try, you always learn something, even if it's from your failures. You learn about yourself and your world. Only through the motivation that gets you to try new things can you gain experience— and experience is one of the best sources of knowledge and wisdom you will ever find.

Commitment

One of the toughest things about getting motivated is committing yourself to staying motivated. The worthwhile things in life often don't come easily or quickly—you will have to commit yourself to doing what it takes, for however long it takes, to achieve your goals.

COMMITMENT, noun.
  1. the act of pledging or engaging oneself
  2. the undertaking of a task
  3. the task itself that one sets oneself to complete

Everyone makes commitments of one kind or another. Some of your commitments are concrete and clear. For example, you have a specific commitment to attending certain classes every day. You know what is expected of you, both for in-class participation and for out-of-class homework assignments. You have a general idea of how long you will have to take those classes. You have friends in class with you with whom you can compare notes on your mutual commitment. You also have an expectation of getting something in return for your commitment: grades, education, and perhaps, in the long run, acceptance to a college, or a good job.

You may also have some commitments that are more open-ended and fuzzy. You may be a committed son or daughter to one or both of your parents. With this type of commitment, your duties and obligations may be less clear. Every family, and even every person, has different ideas about what goes into honoring that kind of commitment. Commitments like that of a child to a parent are often open-ended. They won't end next week, or next year. And you won't always expect a concrete or specific payoff.

I made a commitment as a sophomore in high school that ended up being more involved and drawn-out than I had thought it would be. My friend Madeline talked me into running for student council. I decided the worst that could happen was I'd lose—and since I'd been dealing with a lot of failure that spring, what with being cut from the song-leading group and not making the gymnastic team, I was ready to give it a shot. Madeline ran for vice president and I ran for secretary. I had no clue what the secretary actually did except take notes at meetings. Madeline said we could do whatever we wanted if we got elected.

Once we had committed to running, the nature of that commitment became a bit overwhelming. We made posters, fliers, and buttons, and we developed our own "ticket" to go with our secret "party" (Madeline and I were the party). We also had to give speeches at lunch to the student body about what we would do if we were elected. That was scary, but it forced us to think about how we would commit ourselves to the jobs we sought. On election day, I realized how embarrassed I'd be if we lost. We were running against popular jocks, but I think we won the election because we knew people from all kinds of diverse backgrounds, from the studious yearbook types to the wild pot-smoker types. It was great to win, but the real challenge in the commitment came when we had to set and attain our goals for the next year.

Joanne Ebeling found, in addition to learning teamwork and time management, that basketball boosted her commitment level. "If I was not committed to basketball, I could not have gotten anywhere. I practiced about three hours a day and had games twice a week. I went to the health club and practiced on my own, in the off-season as well as during the season. It took a lot of time. I also spent time at a couple of camps every summer. Being so committed to basketball and constantly striving for the best has helped me with all the tasks I take on—I stay with them until the finish."

List your five most important commitments here:

1. _____

2. _____

3. _____

4. _____

5. _____

Give some thought to the commitments you have now and the commitments you may want to make. Consider the terms. What is required of you? For how long will the commitments last? What, if anything, should you expect in return for your commitment? You will benefit from thinking through your commitments because it will give you a clearer and more realistic view of how you allocate your energy.

On one hand, maybe you haven't focused your energy on that many things and could use a few more commmitments to energize you and help you learn. Maybe a commitment you took on turned out to be not what you wanted, or not as challenging as you thought it would, or you have already met the challenge and need to move on.

On the other hand, you can also overextend yourself to the point where you aren't giving any of your commitments the attention they deserve. Sometimes people just reach for too much, or a commitment will turn out to be more work than was expected. If you find that you've taken on too much, for whatever reason, reassess your commitments. Choose the ones that have priority for you and cut some of the others out. Maggie Debelius, a graduate of St. Agnes School in Virginia who is now at Princeton working on her Ph.D. in English literature, had to do just that. "The summer before my junior year of high school, my parents agreed that I could work in a gallery/shop that sold Asian art and objects—full-time in the summer and then a couple of afternoons a week after school started. The owner was kind of a nut and would never give me a schedule in advance—she just called when she needed me. That was fine for summer but ridiculous once I was back in school. She used to leave messages with my school secretary asking me to work on a particular afternoon. I was into drama and student government and often had my afternoons planned out weeks in advance.

"As it turned out, this didn't work and I had to quit. The commitment had become more than I thought it would be because I never knew when I would have to be there. I had to prioritize, and my school activities were more important to me than the little bit of money I was making. I learned that at any job you should make sure you and your employer are both organized and honest. Make expectations about hours and responsibilities clear from the start."

Staying committed will help you see your dreams and goals through all the rocky steps along the way. It isn't always easy, but when you arrive where you thought you wanted to be all along—or at a new place where you never even imagined you'd be—you'll discover that your hard work was worth it.

· 7 ·

TAKING CARE OF YOURSELF
Staying Healthy and Happy
Inside and Out

I gradually became convinced that it would be a good thing to rent a house in a part of the city where many primitive and actual needs are found . . . [W]hatever perplexities and discouragement concerning the life of the poor were in store for me, I should at least know something at first hand and have the solace of daily activity. I had confidence that although life itself might contain many difficulties, the period of mere passive receptivity had come to an end, and I had at last finished with the everlasting "preparation for life."

JANE ADDAMS
Social worker
1860–1935

For Jane Addams, deciding what she wanted most to do with her life was painfully difficult. For years there seemed to be nothing but wrong answers. She had been born into a life of privilege the year before the Civil War began. Her family's affluence gave Jane the opportunity to receive a comprehensive education, and in 1882 she was a member of the very first graduating class of Rockford College. Yet even with all the knowledge she had gained, she was expected to become a housewife. But Jane knew that, as challenging as motherhood might be, it wasn't for her.

When her father tried to arrange a marriage for her, Jane resisted in every way. She contracted illnesses, some real, some imagined. She traveled to Europe—and then extended her tour for as long as she could. For seven years, Jane struggled with her decision, feeling unsettled and not quite stable.

Finally, after all those years of inner torment, Jane had the opportunity in 1888 to visit Toynbee Hall in London, England. It was a "settlement house" devoted to the needs of the poor. She was fascinated by what she saw. The work seemed captivating and meaningful to her—and she realized that she had found her calling. The next year she returned to Chicago and founded what would become the most famous settlement house of all. It is still standing today and is known simply as Hull House.

Hull House was designed to offer education and guidance to urban immigrant families and others left behind by the nineteenth-century Industrial Revolution. It was a time of great change. While the innovation that came with the large urban factories drew thousands to the cities of America, little attention was given to those unable to find work. There were no laws regarding working conditions, wages, or hours of employment. There were no government social programs. City schools were often inadequate, and there were few charitable societies equipped to deal with this new "urban problem." To help, Hull House was located in the very poorest of neighborhoods. It offered a variety of programs to children and adults alike, and performed what Jane Addams herself would describe as the "humblest of neighborhood services." She was a pioneer in the history of American social welfare. She had found her niche, her place in history, and her happiness and health to boot.

Physical health and mental health are connected to each other— what's going on in your head and heart affects your body, and what's going on in your body affects you mentally. If one isn't up to par, it can drag the other down. You are a whole, the sum of these parts. If you take care of all your parts, the whole will be all that you think it can be.

Physical Health

I must admit that I was no model for physical health, or mental health for that matter, when I was in high school. After I gave up gymnastics, I pretty much stopped exercising, gained weight, and didn't bother to learn any other sports. Had I participated in some sort of regular physical activity such as running, swimming, or playing basketball, it would have done me a world of good. In addition to keeping me physically fit, it would have made me mentally more alert. It wasn't until college that I learned how physical exercise brings about an improved mental state.

Angela Dorn, too, gave up sports after being on the track team her freshman year, and she wishes she had continued. "I regret not being more athletic in high school. I don't think women are encouraged to be 'jocks' like men. It just wasn't that cool." In her case, popular opinion affected her decision not to push herself to stay involved. In my case, I just got lethargic. Either way, we missed out.

Being on any kind of team has the added benefit of the camaraderie you can develop with friends, but any kind of exercise will do you good especially when you combine it with the two other most crucial elements of good physical health: adequate sleep and eating right. Exercise builds the strength of your heart and increases your lung capacity. The more you exercise, the more healthy and strong your muscles and organs become; if you neglect them, they can weaken from disuse. As they say, "Use it or lose it!"

Exercise comes in all forms and styles. You can participate on a team in football, basketball, baseball, track, or field hockey, among others. You can take dance classes or run on your own time. Or you can find exercise in other clubs and groups like scouting organizations, drill team, cheerleading, golf, gymnastics, wrestling, folk dancing, cross-country track, hiking, yoga, martial arts, or aerobics. They all contribute to the fitness of your body.

One advantage to starting to pay attention to fitness now is that you develop a habit, a routine, that has more chance of sticking with you later. I find that now, as a working person with lots of responsibilities at work and outside work, I need to make exercise a priority. If I didn't, I would find it easy to drop from my schedule. As a high school student, you probably have more time to exercise than you ever will after you enter the work force.

"I chose my high school physical activities—dance and field hockey—out of love rather than a desire to stay fit, but now I am glad that exercise was part of my life then, because it naturally became a habit, and these days it can really be a chore to fit it into my schedule," says Sarah Lyman Kravits. "What with my temp jobs, acting auditions, writing work, and traveling from place to place in the city, I am completely swamped. But since I am used to staying in shape, I feel it when I don't exercise—and that gross feeling inspires me to try really hard to fit something in, either a run or some yoga or an aerobics class, at least four times a week, if not more."

Sleep is another key factor in your physical health. Your body needs sleep for gearing up, for repairing, and for resting your busy brain. If you deny yourself sleep, you suffer for it—it's hard to perform to your capacity when you are struggling to stay awake.

Some students get plenty of sleep and rarely let their responsibilities interfere with their sleep schedule. Others push themselves to get everything done no matter how late they have to stay up. "I used to pretend to go to bed, throw one dark sweater over my lamp and put another at the crack of my door, and work on my homework until I was done," confesses Sarah. "I was so driven to do it all—rehearsals, practices, classes, papers, worksheets—that I couldn't even tell when I was getting run-down, I just wondered why I was slowing up."

The secret is to find a middle ground. If you have important tasks to complete, you may have to stay up late or get up early. It won't hurt to have a short night's sleep every once in a while. But if you make sleep a high priority, you won't get worn down. Take each day as it comes, and decide how much you can get done and still get the sleep you need. And when you're beat and you have a little extra afternoon time on your hands, turn off the TV and take a nap! I never appreciated naps as a kid, of course, but now I see what I was missing—they're amazing for restoring energy and getting a fresh start.

The other aspect of physical health that I mentioned is eating habits. Very few people I knew while I was in high school thought too hard about eating right. It's difficult to focus on because you are young and your body seems so invincible and resistant. But believe me, if you have bad habits now, they might come back to haunt you later in life. Annie Wagner, a painter from St. Louis, finds she still gets stuck in her old high school eating habits. "I went to an all-girls school, and we had two food phases—either eating snacks or starving ourselves. We ate whatever was convenient, and snacks were much more convenient than preparing healthy food. I still will go to the deli and get a Snickers bar and a Snapple instead of making something healthy for dinner for myself like I should."

The more you eat right while you're in high school, the healthier and stronger your body will be as it gets older. It gets harder and harder to maintain fitness and a reasonable body weight in later years. If you are used to eating well, you will be able to continue; but if you are used to hamburgers and doughnuts, you will all of a sudden find that it's hard to keep weight down and energy up. So try to eat five servings of fruits and vegetables a day, cut down on fat, and have three meals. You owe it to yourself.

Of course, it's fun to have fast food with your team early in the mornings on game days and leave candy in the locker of your assigned "locker buddy." It's great to stay up late at drama club rehearsals and eat doughnut holes or whatever anybody brings to share. It's fun to go out to the diner after the prom or a dance or party and eat a big meal at one in the morning, or to have ice-cream bars at lunchtime, or, between classes, to eat the chocolate candy you buy from your friend who is selling it to make money for a school club. Just try to squeeze some vegetables and protein and low-fat carbohydrates in between all the other stuff. You'll eventually be glad you did.

Mental Health

Your mental health is connected to, and just as important as, your physical health. High school is a time of change—sometimes you are excited about opening new chapters of your life, and sometimes you are scared. Sometimes you are both at the same time, and that's normal, too. The best things you can do for your mental health right now are to manage the stress in your life and to take advantage of opportunities to have fun.

Managing Stress

As much as you want to get rid of it, stress is a normal part of everyday life.

STRESS, noun.
 a feeling of mental tension and pressure, sometimes affecting physical health, resulting from life's troublesome situations

---

You may feel pressure to get all your homework done, pressure from your friends to go out, pressure from your boss at work to pull an extra shift, or pressure to push yourself to the limit at athletic team practice. Gail Brown, a junior at Manhattan Night Comprehensive High School in New York City, had a school-related stressful situation: "My most stressful situation was convincing the United Negro College Fund not to take away my scholarship. It was in jeopardy because my grades dropped, and on top of that I was pregnant. I handled it by writing each board member a personal letter explaining why he or she should give me a second chance."

Home life can be stressful, too. Perhaps your single mom works and you have to baby-sit after school, or your mom and dad both work late, so you don't get to see them until eight, or maybe you are being raised by a parent or other relative who you don't feel understands you and your needs. "When I was in high school, my dad had a job that kept him away from home for much of the year, but when he was home, he had an intense set of rules," says Rus Blackwell, now an actor in Florida. "I wasn't allowed to leave my stereo on at night or talk for more than five minutes on the phone. Once when I couldn't sleep I put my stereo on softly, and he got up in the middle of the night and hit me. Another time I was on the phone for ten minutes and he knocked it out of my hand. I was stressed out when he was home."

Stressful situations can vary a great deal, but each is serious to the person who experiences it. You have a right to feel stressed, whether it's over the death of a parent or a low grade on a quiz. "One of the most stressful situations that I endured was when I was homeless and my child lived away from me," says Amanda Lee. "I was living with my friend and we got into a fight, and she told me to get out. I moved from place to place; I slept on the train or in the park. The only good thing was that my son stayed with my sister. I struggled, but I got my act together, found someone to live with, and found a job." On the other end of the spectrum is the kind of stress Becky Amato felt from the example set by her parents: "At my high school it is very competitive and there is a great deal of pressure to do well and get into a good college. Not only this, but I am an only child and have been a strong focus for my parents, both of whom are very bright and successful themselves. My greatest fear was to fail academically."

What causes stress? Stress will arise when you feel unsure of what to do, when you fail to achieve a goal you set for yourself, when you think you have done the wrong thing, or when *others* think you have done the wrong thing. Everybody feels stress, no matter how calm or successful they may seem to you. Sometimes the people who seem more pulled together than anyone else look that way because they have to be so organized and controlled to deal with the amount of stress they endure. The President of the United States, for example, is someone who's made it to the top, yet he probably has more stress in his life than anyone else in the country.

Here are some practical steps to help you maintain balance in your life, no matter how tense your circumstances may get.

Identify your stressors.
Free-floating anxiety is harder to deal with than specific problems. You cannot begin to improve a specific situation until you understand what it is.

Write down three of your stressors here:

1. _____

2. _____

3. _____

Categorize your stressors.
There are two kinds of stressful situations: those you can do something about and those you can't. What you can't change, you have to accept and adjust to over time. As for what you *can* change, you can develop a plan of action. For example, here is a stressor I have that I cannot change: my job involves a heavy work load almost all year. Here is one that I can change (and did): I was living with an apartment-mate with whom I wasn't getting along, and I took the initiative and moved out to a one-bedroom on my own.

Look at the stressors you listed above. Decide here if each is something you can change or something unchangeable to which you must adjust. Write "change" or "adjust" for each.

1. _____

2. _____

3. _____

Develop that action plan.
For those things you can change, think through and write down the positive steps you can take to improve the situation. Thinking and writing will give you a degree of comfort and relief even before you take action—you'll know that you're on your way to making a change. For those you cannot change, write down what you can do to alleviate the stress that the situation causes. It may relate to the stress directly, or it may be something completely different that helps you relax, such as exercise or quiet time. Here are my action plans for the worries I described above:

1. Heavy work load at job
   Actions: a. Take 10 minutes each morning to plan day for maximum efficiency.

b. Spend some extra time—a half-day each weekend—getting caught up.
2. Roommate problem
    Actions: a. Decide to move out.
              b. Locate new single-occupancy apartment.
              c. Find new apartment-mate to take my old room.
              d. Move.

How about your actions? Write here what action you can take to reduce your stressors.

1. Stressor _____

   Actions _____

   _____

   _____

2. Stressor _____

   Actions _____

   _____

   _____

3. Stressor _____

   Actions _____

   _____

   _____

Give yourself breathing time.
It's good to set aside time each day for fifteen minutes or half an hour just to be quiet, to be alone with your thoughts. Some people may pray, some may meditate, others may just sit and think. The important thing is that it is time for you and you alone. You may find it easier

to work through problems if you allow yourself some quiet, unfocused relaxation time.

When in your day can you fit in some quiet time? _____

How do you think it may reduce your specific stressors? _____

_____

Exercise three to five times a week.
Exercise is one of the best ways to manage stress. Whether you ride your bike, play basketball, or jog, exercise helps you to feel better about yourself. Why? For one, it improves your overall health, and that in turn improves your appearance. Also, when you exercise, your body releases chemicals called endorphins, which are a natural energy boost and mood elevator. Plus, stress often manifests itself as muscle tension. Exercise helps to release that physical sign of stress; the feeling of reducing muscle tension often helps to release mental tension as well. James Morris finds release in his football playing: "During the school year I practice both before and after school, and three hours a day during the summer. Football relaxes me in a way. It gets my mind off the other pressures that I have. It's a challenge."

What kinds of exercise do you like? _____

When do you find time to exercise? _____

What kinds of stress can exercise help you release? _____

_____

_____

Take advantage of your counselors and teachers.
Your high school has qualified personnel who are there to help you cope with all kinds of stress and confusion. Look for help when you need it. These people are your resources, and they've helped others through all kinds of problems. Chances are they can help you, too.

Do you think any of your stressors might be reduced with help from a teacher or counselor? If so, what are they? How might the person help you?

_____

_____

_____

_____

Take time out for your favorite relaxers.
Do you love listening to music? Taking a walk? Talking things over with a good friend? Dancing? Writing? Going for a drive? Anything that helps to relax you will relax your mind as well. Mental downtime is good for you because your brain can focus better when it is relaxed. Also, problems can look different after you have taken yourself away from them for a while. You may find you come up with new ideas after a period of relaxation. Floris Suarez has three favorite relaxers: "When I'm stressed I usually go out for a walk, or I'll speak about it to my friend Maribell. Sometimes I listen to music and try to calm myself down."

What are your favorite relaxing things to do?

1. _____

2. _____

3. _____

When working with stressful situations, be gentle with yourself. This is a time of gradual transition, and change often happens slowly, or in fits and starts, rather than overnight.

Finding the Fun

One of the most important things in high school—and in life—is finding and doing whatever you think is fun. Not only does fun reduce your stress level, it makes life worthwhile. I had no problem having fun in high school. I could always find a way to entertain myself. My challenge was in finding the discipline I needed to adequately challenge and direct my energies.

As soon as I stopped viewing high school as an institution of fear and repression and opened my mind, I began to see it as a real opportunity. Every day I was learning more about myself and the world. Seeing high school as an opportunity enabled me to have fun learning, instead of viewing it as some arduous chore.

All kinds of things, from the regular to the ridiculous, can be fun. Everyone has their own ideas of what is enjoyable to do. Sometimes you have fun doing things that you are good at. "I like to sing," says Gail Brown. "Singing and running track are my best talents. I sing all the time. I was in a school talent show and won first place." But you can have fun doing things that don't especially require talent either. David Rowe had the most fun socializing with his local friends: "Socializing was perhaps the most important thing to me in high school. We went to a lot of parties, to the movies, and to the beach. I still love to socialize."

Reading is another source of fun. For the most part, the more you like what you read, the more you get out of it. Patrick Weisel, a painter in New York City, enjoyed reading Shakespeare and Edgar Allan Poe. "They were the only books that no one checked out of the library, so I decided I'd be the one to read them—I thought they must be sophisticated. They gave me a base of knowledge that has been important to me." Garth Kravits loved *Mad* magazine. "I felt adult when I read that kind of subtle, almost taboo humor. It had a lot of wordplay that made me feel like I was reading something more grownup than the Sunday comics. I always loved reading things that were funny, even though they weren't usually what was assigned in class."

TV, movies, and shows are popular sources of entertainment. Melissa Rekas makes them part of her social time. "When we can afford it, my friends and I go to see movies. We also rent out movies and watch them at each other's houses, because it's cheaper and we can hang out and make a lot of popcorn. It's also fun to go to see the shows at the other high schools around our area."

Group activities, such as sports, clubs, scouting groups, or drama, art, or music groups, can be great, too. Deena Mottola enjoyed singing with a choir. "I was in the choir during the entire four years of high school. We traveled a lot and went to state meets in Boston, Montreal, and Virginia Beach. It was really a lot of fun because we got to get away from our parents for a while. The best thing about choir was that I formed some of my deepest friendships in this group. We were traveling together, studying together, and living together!''

Whatever you think is fun, whether it's hanging out in the mall with your friends or knitting or lying out in the sun at lunch hour or collecting stamps or talking on the phone or writing poems or drawing or making mix tapes, find time for it. "Sometimes it's hard to find time for fun with all the schoolwork and my job, but I manage to fit it in,'' says Melissa. "School dances like Homecoming are fun. Once a friend and I rented a paddle boat and rode it to the middle of Centennial Lake and sang songs. Also I like to go to this little town near us and look through all of the shops there. Sometimes I like to play pool, when we go to a friend's house where there is a pool table. Or we can always just drive around.''

"I like to go coffee-shop hopping,'' says Andy Wardlaw, a classmate of Melissa's. "Camping is great, too, and writing and playing music with my band—lots of people form their own bands.''

Alcohol, Cigarettes, and Drugs

Students today are likely to encounter one or more of these substances at some point during high school. Many people, although not all, experiment with all three while in high school. They're around—that's just how the world is these days. But using them isn't really a good idea. Although alcohol can be a normal part of life when consumed in reasonable amounts on social occasions, in large quantities it can cause problems for your health. And in any amount, cigarettes and drugs are harmful to you.

Not everyone around you will set a good example. Friends, parents, and other authority figures may smoke or drink too much. If you see it a lot, it may seem normal, although your gut feelings may tell you it isn't quite right. Eric Davis of Burlington, Massachusetts, learned the hard way to listen to his second thoughts. "It was a Friday morning and we didn't have school because of a teachers' conference. One of my friends had gotten the key to his family's beach house in New Hampshire. The word got out and about fifty people drove there. When we got to the house, another of my friends went to a couple of stores—the first one wouldn't sell him anything, but the second did, and he came back with twelve cases of beer. People began drinking, and before anyone noticed, everyone was on the beach, the roof, and the neighbors' property.

"Needless to say, the police came and took fourteen guys to the station. They called our parents and asked them to come and pick us up. At that point I started to get really scared. We all acted like total idiots and could have gotten in even bigger trouble or, worse, ended up dead. But later I realized that I had to start becoming responsible for my actions. I know now that my parents aren't always going to be there to get me out of trouble."

When your friends abuse alcohol or drugs, at least you have some power to disassociate yourself from them; but when the problem occurs at home, it's harder to escape. Some of you may have mothers, fathers, or siblings who abuse alcohol or drugs. Problems can range from one too many drinks each night before dinner to crack addiction to dealing drugs for profit. Sometimes family members will abuse a substance and keep to themselves; other times, under the substance's effect, they can hurt others physically or emotionally through their words and actions. Abusers may get into trouble with drugs or alcohol once a day or once a month. The situations can vary immensely, but the bottom line is, substance abuse in your family hurts you.

What does it do to you? It can make you feel as if something you do has caused the abuse. It can lead to your being neglected and ignored. It can make you wonder why someone whom you love and who you think loves you could cause you so much pain. It can cause situations where your physical health and well-being are in danger. It can create chilly distance between you and the abuser. It can make you feel alone, unloved, useless, disturbed, angry, sad, and depressed.

How do you deal with this problem? The first step is to realize what you can and cannot control. *You cannot control a parent's or sibling's behavior*—alcohol and drug abuse is something people have to come to terms with on their own, and for the right reasons (to heal themselves, to find a clear head, to face up to what problems they have caused and how to mend them honestly). On the other hand, *you DO have some control over your own life*—what you do, where you go, and how you perceive the problem. Focus on making a healthy life for yourself by trying out the following tactics:

- Attend meetings at a family support group such as Al-Anon.
- Attend student support meetings at your school.

- Catch your family member in a clean and sober moment and tell him or her how you feel.
- If living at home is threatening your safety because of the abuser's behavior or friends of the abuser who threaten you, find a place to stay with a friend or another relative.
- Realize that your family member's behavior stems from the substance abuse and not necessarily from dislike of you (in other words, it's not your fault!).
- Talk to your counselor at school.
- Make choices to live your own life differently.

Sometimes a dangerous home life doesn't look so dangerous at all. Families of heavy drinkers can sometimes quietly encourage problem drinking. Do people in your family regularly drink until they are out of control? Do they drink every day? Does a parent encourage you to drink to prove your maturity? Do your parents not care if you raid the liquor cabinet? Although these conditions don't necessarily create problem drinking automatically, they can foster an environment where it can grow more easily.

Be wary of your family's attitude toward drinking. If your parents set an abusive example, even if they tell you to do as they say and not as they do, you may have registered their behavior as normal in your mind. Your best bet is to follow your instincts. If you have any feeling that how your family lives isn't quite how you want to or should live, follow that hunch and see where it leads you. Chances are it will bring you to a place where you are comfortable and healthier than you would have been otherwise.

Sometimes you will make your own choice to try something, but other times you will do it because people encourage you to. When your individual values and goals are different from your family, the group you hang with, or even just one of your friends, you may feel pressure to do something against your will. It's easy to become excited by what everyone else is excited about doing, even if it isn't exactly a smart move. Be cautious. Use your head.

One of the best ways to know whether you should or should not do something that your peers are encouraging you to do is to follow your own gut feelings. If you feel at all that something might be a bad idea, if you have any sense of dread, if you wish secretly that your parents would tell you that you couldn't do a certain activity or go to a certain party, then listen to yourself. You have the best shot at keeping your own best interests at heart. Even when your friends mean well by inviting you to try something, it is impossible for them to see inside your mind and know what you are thinking. Everyone is different, and what a friend may think is a fun or necessary activity for him- or herself is not necessarily right for you.

Tamika Leslie got herself out of a situation that she entered into because her friends wanted her to join them: "I can't stand to be in groups where one person decides what the rest of the group does even if they don't want to. I had an experience like that, and I promised myself that I will never again do something I don't want to do. I went to a party with some girls one night. I didn't want to go—I wanted to go to another party. I went anyway, and just when we started having fun, they started shooting up drugs right there. I left them and went home."

Sticking up for what you want to do when your friends want you to do something else is not easy. Do your best, and if and when you do something you regret, just take time to think about what you can learn from it. Any experience from which you can take some wisdom is never wasted, as John Zora found out. "My parents always warned me not to drive with somebody who was under the influence of alcohol. I never really followed their advice because I saw my friends drive drunk without any problem, although I always wondered how they could do it without crashing into anything. Well, on August 24, 1993, I found out there is always that 'one time' when fate may not be in your favor.

"My friend Tony had a party, and we were both drinking. He asked me to go to our local swim club with him, just five minutes away. Deciding to go was the biggest mistake I have made in my entire life. He drove his Camaro 70 mph in a 25 mph zone. Suddenly he lost control and we crashed into a parked car. He wasn't wearing his seat belt and he flew out the front window. I had my seat belt on, so I stayed in the car as it continued moving and hit a telephone pole. When the car stopped, I got out and saw Tony with blood covering his whole body. The ambulance came and took him to the hospital—he lived but needed eighty stitches. I had a CAT scan but luckily was all right. Tony lost his license for six months, and his insurance went up dramatically.

"My parents were ashamed of me because I let them down—I embarrassed them as well as myself. Because of this incident I will never drive drunk, and my friends and I make sure we have a designated driver when we go out. I will never take anything for granted in life again because I know that fate isn't always on your side."

Not all friends will push you to do things you don't want to do. David Rowe used to hang with a group who did the opposite. "When I was in high school, we went to parties practically every Saturday night. We all had to make choices about drinking and drugs because they were around all the time. What was great about my friends was that they provided a lot of peer pressure to keep you in line. If you got really messed up or did something stupid, they gave you a hard time. One night I stayed out all night, and when I was driving home I totaled my parents' car. I hadn't even been drinking, but I got really sleepy and fell asleep at the wheel. My parents didn't give me a hard time because they were relieved I was not hurt. But my friends let me know how stupid I was for driving when I was so tired." This was a group of friends who really cared about one another in an honest, smart way.

Inevitably, at some time during high school, you will be invited to a party where there is alcohol and, perhaps, drugs. Before you go headfirst into experimenting with them, think through the pros and cons. Let's say you go to a party and have a couple of beers. If you walk home, get a ride from a non-drinking designated-driver friend, or stop drinking and wait one hour for each drink you had before you drive home, you may be safe. A study quoted in a book published by the American Academy of Pediatrics states that 15 percent of high school seniors have driven while intoxicated; per year, 7,000 teenagers are killed and 40,000 injured. Don't add to this somber statistic.

Cigarettes may seem less obviously harmful because they don't impair your brain processes in the same way that alcohol and drugs can do. But they are a true danger to your health. Cigarette smoking, as well as chewing tobacco, can cause cancer of the mouth, throat, and lungs. Nicotine, the drug tobacco contains, dilates your blood vessels and can speed up your heart rate; your body can become addicted to this drug over time and give you the impression that you "need" it. The more you use it, the harder it becomes to kick the habit, and the longer you smoke or chew, the greater your chances of developing a life-threatening disease.

Smoking causes different problems for different people. Athletes and other sports-minded people may find that smoking reduces their lung capacity and hampers their performance in their favorite sport. Singers, actors, and others who rely on their voices may discover that smoking damages their delicate vocal cords and causes their voices to change and/or lose power. For women, smoking can lead to problems in pregnancy such as a low-birth-weight baby, inability to carry the baby to term, and birth defects. Smoking may seem cool, but in the long run it just isn't worth it.

As for drugs, they are illegal for a reason—they cause harm to your brain and body. Unless you want to risk your future and your health, you should avoid them and the people who offer them to you. You will be far more cool in the long run if you learn to use your mind, your imagination, and your creative spirit to make your life thrilling and meaningful without artificial substances. Speak up for yourself and stand your ground.

Melissa Rekas offers advice about how she deals with her peers. "When people that I know drink or smoke pot or anything else, I just don't hang around with them while they do it. I can't change their values, but they won't change mine, either. One friend of mine has gotten himself out of a bad alcohol problem, and he always says, 'It's stupid to drink because it tastes weird, you act dumb, you don't know what you're doing, and then the next morning you have a huge headache. What's fun about that?' We also have two school organizations that help students and make everyone aware—SHOP (Students Helping Other People) and SADD (Students Against Drunk Driving). They offer counseling through the health center, and we do community service."

Drugs can lead to some chilling and violent experiences. Gail Brown learned the hard way about life around drugs. "My best friend, who happened to have been a drug dealer, was killed by his own friends. They set him up and shot him five times in the head because he was the boss and was making more money than all of them. I've come to realize that your friends can turn on you, and that if you are always playing around with drugs and things, you won't really pay attention to things around you affecting your life."

Accidents can happen so easily, even when you're making an effort to do the right thing. "One night, when I was a sophomore in high school, a good friend of mine named Doug was out drinking with some guys, including my boyfriend," says Kimberly Diamond of Somerville, Massachusetts. "Dougie had his car with him, and none of the guys knew that he had expected to drive home. So when he went to get into his car they tried to stop him. My boyfriend got into a fight with him because he wouldn't give up his keys. He went speeding off, and no one heard from him until they found out he was in the hospital— he had lost control on the highway in the rain and flipped over. He was unconscious and had to get stitches in his head. After that I told myself I would never drink and drive. It made me realize how precious life is—I would never risk my life or the lives of others over something so ridiculous."

Anything you do that doesn't take into account the value of life can bring tragedy upon you. There are enough difficulties in life without bringing substance abuse in to make things worse. If you experiment with substances, all I ask is that you also try some drug- and alcohol-free experiences that can challenge you. The best high is the one you get from working hard to achieve a goal you've set for yourself and putting your heart and soul into something you value.

Sexual Issues

As much attention as sex gets, quite a few high school students are not sexually active. If you are one of them, you are not abnormal or a prude or hopelessly behind. You have simply made a choice that seems best for your life and your values right now. If it seems to you as if there aren't too many virgins around, it is usually because very few people brag about being a virgin—it doesn't seem as cool as being experienced. Whatever your attitudes about sex, if you have doubts and questions, it is best to talk to an adult that you trust, preferably a counselor or a doctor; that way you will receive the most reliable, up-to-date, honest information possible.

Sex is something that should not be taken lightly; it can have some damaging consequences. If you feel pressure to have sex against your will from a boyfriend or girlfriend, stick to what makes sense for you. If you have any doubts, it is better to just say no. Some people would break up with you in that situation. So be it. Wouldn't you rather go out with someone who respects and values what is important to you? You will find someone who puts your values and needs first—he or she will be worth the wait.

Sometimes people become victims of sexual violence, more often women than men. It's important to be aware of potential danger. Cynthia Nordberg had a frightening encounter with date rape, many years before it was recognized as a problem in society. "This guy was a star athlete at my high school, and very good-looking. I wasn't in love with him, but I was in love with being popular, and going out with him made any girl look good. On our third date, we went to a party, and after only ten minutes he wanted to go get some dessert. I didn't really want to leave my friends, and I didn't like how quiet he seemed, but I wanted to please him, so we went. We got in the car, and he drove the opposite direction from town. When I asked him where we were going, he didn't answer and just turned up the radio full blast. I kept telling myself not to panic, but I knew something was brewing.

"He parked in the desert in a secluded area. No one was around, and it was pitch-dark. He started kissing me and became really forceful. I kept saying no and trying to sit up, but he overpowered me. He pulled out a condom and raped me, as my mind repeated no over and over again. It was the most humiliating experience of my life. Every day at school he acted like nothing had happened. Finally I broke down in the bathroom and told my best friend everything. She told me to tell the police, but I thought it was too late and didn't feel that anyone would believe me. I learned from this incident that I should always trust my gut instincts—I never should have left the party. Now, when I feel uneasy about something, a red flag goes up and I stop and think. It has saved me from other costly mistakes. I also learned that self-respect is more important than being popular. Trusting and respecting yourself is critical to making sound decisions in every area of your life."

Abstaining from sex altogether, or practicing safe sex using birth control, has two major benefits for you. One is protection against the incurable disease of AIDS, a growing epidemic in the United States and around the world. The human immunodeficiency virus (HIV), transmitted through unprotected sex, intravenous drug use, and upon rare occasions by medical procedures involving contaminated blood, gradually weakens the immune system, and AIDS results. The body, no longer able to fight against invading germs, then succumbs to diseases like pneumonia or other viruses that normally would be destroyed by the immune system or controlled by medication. At this time, there is no prognosis for AIDS patients other than a gradual decline and eventual death. The best and safest way to prevent AIDS is *to abstain*.

Jeremy Kaber of Cherry Hill, New Jersey, took a family living class in high school that educated him about the AIDS virus. "The occurrence that affected me the most was when our teacher brought in a speaker—a young man in his twenties, a graduate of my high school, who had HIV. He told us the story of how he became exposed to the disease through unsafe sex, and warned us to avoid the same mistakes that he is now suffering from. Many of us had believed that this could never happen to us, that we would be safe—but we realized that this was obviously untrue because the reality of this illness was standing right in front of us."

Although AIDS gets most of the attention these days, don't forget that the other sexually transmitted diseases (STDs) that have been around for centuries are still doing damage. Unprotected sex with someone whose history is a mystery to you could result in your contracting gonorrhea, herpes, chlamydia, syphilis, or other diseases that range from annoying to life-threatening. Some newer strains have even developed a resistance to the drugs that have been traditionally used in treatment, and some diseases, such as herpes, are never completely curable. Protect yourself from having to deal with this issue! However, if you find you have been exposed to or are suffering from an STD, see a doctor right away—your health depends on it.

The other benefit of abstention or practicing safe sex is that you avoid becoming pregnant (or, in the case of the guys, contributing to a pregnancy). Having a child is a gigantic step that changes your life and piles on tons of responsibilities that don't go away anytime soon. I have strong feelings on this issue because I've seen some of the traumatic effects that unwanted pregnancies have had on a few friends. One of my friends became pregnant her senior year of high school and had an abortion. It was a painful experience that will stay with her for the rest of her life. Another friend of mine got his girlfriend pregnant, and they married at eighteen and had the baby. Although the couple loved their child, it was tough for the father to handle a pre-med course load at college while working two jobs to support the family. Several years later they divorced, in part because they had little in common other than their child.

Still another friend of mine chose to have her baby and raised her as a single mother. Five years later, she fell in love and married, but she had a lot of pain and hardship during those five years on her own. Even though raising a child can be one of the most rewarding experiences you'll ever have, it is also one of the most challenging, difficult, and exhausting, and it is much easier to divide the duties and responsibilities with a spouse. Plus, when you are older, your life is more settled; focusing on childrearing at that time will probably fit in better with your lifestyle.

The consequences of the steps you take now can affect the whole course of your life. Take the time to think things through and try not to succumb to peer pressure. You will be an adult for at least three-quarters of your life, so don't be in a hurry to get there. Gail Brown found out how she felt about being pregnant when it happened to her. "I got pregnant when I was fifteen and a half, and for a while I felt like my life was over. I don't want my daughter to have to struggle as I do. I want her to be able to enjoy her childhood without having to take care of a child." Gail discovered that parenthood will make you grow up awfully fast.

You have only one you! Taking care of your health in every way, inside and out, will help you make the most of life. Some people, like Syracuse, New York, college student Bryan Kenny, find out about life's value in a way that really sticks. "One night, my friend and I were driving along the back roads heading to nowhere in particular. I was ahead of her and had a faster car, and soon I noticed that she wasn't behind me anymore. I went to the end of the road, figuring she had found a shortcut and would meet me there, but she wasn't there. I knew something was wrong—my stomach began to turn.

"I drove back the way I came, and just as I turned a corner I saw her car engulfed in flames. I feared the worst—that she was dead. I ran over to the car in disbelief, and everything turned to complete confusion. I had to help her! Then I heard someone faintly call my name. There she was along the side of the road—somehow she had made it out of the car after it hit a tree and went halfway down the hill. She was lucky to be alive. This experience made me realize the value of life and how quickly it could be taken from you. Since then I have become more mature and responsible. I try to be healthy and active and live life to the fullest."

PART THREE

EXPANDING YOUR WORLD

• 8 •

GETTING HIRED,
GETTING ACCEPTED
Applying for Jobs and to Colleges

I had scarcely passed my twelfth birthday when I entered the inhospitable regions of examinations, through which for the next seven years I was destined to journey. These examinations were a great trial for me. The subjects which were dearest to the examiners were almost invariably those I fancied least.   WINSTON CHURCHILL
                                                    Statesman
                                                    1874–1965

In high school, no one was a poorer student than Winston Churchill. At Harrow, where he was enrolled, the students were grouped in several "forms" according to their academic ability. Churchill, a poor student and a disciplinary problem, was in the lowest form. Even within that group he was last in his class. Although it was standard practice during this era in England to teach all college-bound students Latin and Greek, his teachers had him focus on a more basic subject, English composition, because they thought he should prepare for a "practical" career. Churchill did apply to the two most choice universities, Oxford and Cambridge, but didn't get in. Instead, he enrolled in a military academy called Sandhurst and joined the Army.

By the time he took his first tour of duty, Churchill had seen enough of the world to arouse his own ambitions for achievement. Realizing that he hadn't planned well for his future when he didn't make the most of school, he decided to educate himself. With the extra time he had on his hands at his lonely military outpost in India, he read any book he could get his hands on—Aristotle, Plato, and other philosophers; fiction; and volumes of parliamentary debates.

In time, his work and dedication paid off. He developed a solid

151

appreciation for reading and writing. He gained a love for just talking to people at the dinner table, even as his food got cold, and that later fed his affinity for speechmaking. He became a master of what he did learn in school: communication and skillful use of the English language. Politics was his next logical career direction. He got the opportunity after a daring exploit drew national attention: as a journalist covering the Boer War in South Africa, he had been taken prisoner, escaped, and was able to make his way over three hundred miles of enemy territory to freedom. Knowing a good opportunity when he saw one, he ran for Parliament and was elected. He became a national figure and an expert in military affairs.

In World War II, Britain faced its worst crisis ever as the Nazis, led by Adolf Hitler, overran the Continent of Europe. In this crisis—as Britain stood almost alone against Hitler, facing the threat of German invasion—what the country needed most was a leader capable of inspiring it and communicating its needs to the outside world. So Britain turned to Winston Churchill, who became its Prime Minister. Some of his inspiring words:

> *Even though large tracts of Europe and many old and famous states have fallen or may fall into the grip of the Gestapo and all the odious apparatus of Nazi rule, we shall not flag or fail. We shall go on to the end. We shall fight in France, we shall fight on the seas and oceans, we shall fight with growing confidence and growing strength in the air, we shall defend our island, whatever the cost may be, we shall fight on the beaches, we shall fight on the landing grounds, we shall fight in the fields and the streets, we shall fight in the hills; we shall never surrender.*

Winston Churchill is an excellent example of someone making the most of his abilities and resources. He got to know himself and made choices that made sense for who he was and what he could do. You don't need to become a famous prime minister, of course. You just need to do right by yourself and find what suits you best.

Making Plans That Fit You

Whether you are looking for a part-time job, preparing to apply to colleges, or getting ready to enter the work force after high school graduation, the first step is to decide what plan suits your needs. This isn't easy, but any decision is the right one as long as it fits you. Some people work during school, some work only during the summer, and some don't work at all. Some people go right to college, some go right to work, and some work for a few years and then attend college, using their work years to save money and to decide exactly what course of study they want to pursue. And some go to college for a couple of years and then drop out to enter the work force. You have a lot of options!

If you are looking for a job while you are still in high school, your first move is to decide what you want and need in a job. Here are some considerations you might have. Make a note about what you want in each category.

- **Job purpose—interest or money.** Do you want to work at something you are interested in pursuing as a career, or do you just want something that will earn you some decent cash? If you want a combination of the two, know which is your priority in case you can't find the ideal job.

- **Pay.** How much money do you want to make? Different jobs will earn you different-size paychecks. If you need money to help your family or to raise a child, you might need a higher-paying job. If you just want extra dollars for movies, clothing, and CDs, money might not be as much of a concern. Most jobs you will find, since they are primarily part-time, pay by the hour.

- **Time frame.** Do you want to work during school or during the summer? Do you want part-time work or full-time (summer only)? Does your school have a co-op program that allows you to alternate work weeks and school weeks? Do you want to work weekday evenings or weekends?

- **Type of job.** Do you want to prepare or sell food, answer phones, sell retail, clean homes or malls or offices, work as a lifeguard, teach or baby-sit kids, operate computers, work at a movie theater, garage, or flower shop? There are lots of options, depending on what's around your area.

- **Location.** How do you plan to get to work—can you walk, do you have a car, can someone drive you, or do you need public transportation? Take your mode of travel into account. Also, you may want to work in an area near your school or neighborhood so that you can save time traveling to and from all of your activities.

I wanted to be a nurse when I started high school; my grandmother had been one, and nursing was one of the few careers I knew about. My guidance counselor said that if I wanted to be a nurse I should find out ahead of time if I could deal with death, and she suggested I volunteer at a hospice, a place that cares for terminally ill patients who don't have long to live. So I signed up. It took all my courage to go through the four-week training program on death and dying, and when I was ready to begin work, I was terrified. So far in my lifetime, no one in my immediate family had ever died. I hoped I could keep my cool and help the patients.

I worked two days a week all summer between my sophomore and junior years. It was tough because I became attached to the patients— Candace asked me to read to her, Vivian used to own a beauty parlor and had me paint her nails, Raymond would drink beer and watch sports and had no use for me, and John just wanted me to sit and tell him about what it was like to be fifteen. I never got used to the fact that these people whom I was close to eventually died. It made a lasting impression on me. Some days I would arrive and one bed would be empty. It was hard to accept, but I felt I had at least helped to make their remaining time more enjoyable. I really began to understand how not to take anyone in my life for granted—these people could be my parents, my brothers, my cousins, or my friends. The value of life became obvious to me.

After I discovered that I had the courage to deal with life and death, I thought I was definitely cut out to be a nurse—until I ran into trouble in chemistry and physics! Sciences were never my strength, and when I had a hard time in those classes, I knew I needed to reevaluate my career choice. Eventually, I kept the impulse to help others and dropped the idea that I had to help in a scientific environment. It just goes to show that on the way to something you think you want, you often make valuable self-discoveries and take new paths you never even knew existed.

For those of you wondering whether to work or to continue your studies after you graduate, you need to consider your personal financial needs, your family's finances, the career you want to pursue, and how much school or training it requires. You also need to know if you are ready to continue school or if you need a break, weighing the responsibility and independence of work versus the challenging but less "real world" environment of college.

If you decide to move on to college, here are some additional factors for your decision-making process. Again, list your preferences below each paragraph.

- **Money.** Cost is a big issue for almost everyone, because college isn't cheap. If money isn't a problem, you're a lucky soul and can go to any school that accepts you. For everyone else, think about how you can afford your education. Can your family take out a loan? Are you eligible for any government grants or student loans? Can you opt for a community college, or a state college if you are a resident of that state? Can you go to a commuter college and save boarding costs? What scholarships are available to you?

- **Degree and length of study.** Depending on what you want to do, you may need two, four, six, seven, or more years of study. If you want to be a doctor, count on at least eleven including your residency; for a lawyer, seven; a businessperson with an MBA, six; undergraduate degree, four; associate degree or technical/business school certificate, two. More years of school aren't necessarily better if you don't want to pursue a career that requires that much study. Think generally about what you want to pursue, and follow the path that gives you the education you need.

- **Location.** Money often affects this decision. A nearby college to which you commute from home or which charges you in-state tuition will help ease the financial strain. Or you may want to experience a different part of the country, build your independence by going to school far from your family, or experience a new environment like the city or country, a large or small school.

- **Course of study.** What do you want to do? Most people don't really know until maybe their third year of college, when they have to declare a major. But if you have a general idea, you can look into schools that are known for strong departments in your area of interest.

Information Gathering

The next step is to gather information that will help you find the job or college that you want. You have a wide variety of resources available to you, both written and human.

Written Resources

When you are looking for a job, either during school or after graduation, your best written resource is the Help Wanted section in the newspaper. Every day it lists hundreds or thousands of jobs. At the beginning of the section, you will find a guide to the different categories of job listing and the pages where you can find them. If you have already gotten a good idea of what you want, you will be able to sort through the listings and come up with a few options.

Other written resources include bulletin boards at your school guidance office or in your neighborhood café or shopping center. Jobs doing everything from mowing lawns to baby-sitting to computer programming can be posted on a bulletin board. Also, many businesses post a HELP WANTED sign outside when looking for new employees. Take time to check boards or postings when you pass by. Jim Lindsey had luck with a HELP WANTED sign at a McDonald's: "I saw a sign, put in an application for the hell of it, and poof, there I was with a job!"

Whether or not you are currently looking for a job, find two jobs in the newspaper or on a board that suit your needs and wants. List them here. And for the future, get yourself a little notebook in which you can keep track of your job hunting by writing down all the names and addresses of your job contacts, pasting in any classified ads that you answer, and noting your progress.

Job: _____

Source: _____

Contact person: _____

Phone number: _____

Any other information listed (salary, hours, days, duties, skill requirements, experience):

_____

_____

_____

Job: _____

Source: _____

Contact person: _____

Phone number: _____

Any other information listed (salary, hours, days, duties, skill requirements, experience):

_____

_____

_____

Networking: The Human Resource

David Rowe's knack for making friends has led to career success. "I work at a gallery as an art historian specializing in ethnographic and historic antiquities, I own and manage an apartment building, and I chair the local crime and safety committee. In the art world, a lot of business is done through relationships. People will buy from you if they know you and trust you. Good social skills are essential at receptions and openings. By meeting all the important movers and shakers in my community, I can make a difference where I live. My ability to socialize has taught me subtle skills such as diplomacy, which is important in the local political scene, and judging character from conversation, which a landlord needs in order to avoid renting to problem tenants."

NETWORK, verb.
   1. to introduce oneself to another to promote something
   2. to make a contact for an immediate or future purpose

Networking means taking advantage of the human resources in your life—friends, family, teachers, counselors, coaches, community members, and so on. In order to make and maintain contacts and eventually find opportunities through them, you'll need to take an honest interest in others and follow through on that interest by listening, doing favors for them, and just being a reliable friend. If you show interest in people, they will be more likely to feel inclined to do the same for you.

You probably already have networking skills that you use with your circle of friends. Without knowing it, I experienced the value of networking early on—I used it to find a date to my prom! I had kept in touch with a friend from camp, and when prom time came around and I didn't have anyone at school that I wanted to go with, I went with my camp friend, who lived in another town. The more you build your base of friends and contacts, the more it will help you later on, whether you need a job, college advice, or a date.

When you are looking for a job, people come in handy. High school students most often find work through friends or family members. Heather Pollack found her movie theater job through friends. Baby-sitting jobs often come from mothers that you know in the neighborhood. Parents have friends who need help in their offices or restaurants. Shaun Crawford got a boost from a relative. "My aunt hired me to work in her candy store, and it taught me a lot about responsibility. The store is in our kitchen off the back porch. She lets me open the store, deal with customers, and count the money. Some kids smart off to you a lot so I've had to learn to be courteous even when I feel like going off on them."

Some of the contacts you make now will continue to help you in the future. The networking that Sarah Lyman Kravits does stretches back to high school. "I have stayed in touch with my high school drama teacher since graduation ten years ago. He has quite a few success stories in the hundreds of students he has taught and directed over the years, and one person in particular became a casting director. He brought her in to talk to us when I was a senior. I kept in touch with her, and when I moved to New York, not only did she give me valuable advice about my résumé and photo, she also helped me introduce myself by mail to a couple of soap opera casting offices. I still let her know what I'm doing—you never know."

Heather makes connections now much in the way she did as a student. "Sometimes we joke that the film industry is 'high school with money' because there are little cliques. For instance, in my wardrobe union, if for your first job you are hired by a supervisor in a certain group, you are pegged right away as part of that group and no other group will hire you. This happened to me! Luckily, I had made friends with someone from another clique who convinced her supervisor to give my work a chance. Now lots of groups will all hire me and I rarely have trouble getting work. I think this is because of my ability to make friends and network with them—which is extremely important when you free-lance. People will hire you if they like you, because they have to spend so many hours with you."

The payoff from networking can be unpredictable. Sandra McCullough had that experience. "I was working at my local community center. I enjoyed myself and did my job well, and I guess they liked me, because through them I ended up at another job. They told me about it, recommended me for it, and helped me apply. I interviewed for the job, as a receptionist in the state office building in a senator's office, and I got it. I greeted people and answered telephones, among other things. I got to meet new people and have new experiences, and I was successful at what I did." Sandra will probably find that the connections she's making at this job will lead her to even more opportunities in the future.

Networking can also help you with decisions about college. An older friend may attend a college that interests you, and can give you the lowdown, or perhaps someone will start you thinking about a school you hadn't considered. Sarah found her college through a bizarre sequence of events. "The summer before my senior year I hung out at a certain pool because I had a thing for one of the lifeguards who had done a show with me at my school. He blew me off by setting me up with another lifeguard. I was furious, but the other guy was good-looking and nice, so we went out a few times. He talked a lot about college—he was in his second year—and when he found out I had no clue where to go, he recommended his school. He had a scholarship, and I really wanted to try for one, too, to help my parents out. That fall, when I found out my school didn't have an application for the scholarship, I called him and he got the college to send one—and there I was the next fall, at the same college, on the same scholarship."

Think of three people who are close to you; they can be friends, family members, teachers, bosses, anyone you talk to and trust. Have you ever discussed your goals with these people? Talk to each person and see if they have any advice for you about how to follow your dreams or about contacts who might be able to help you. You may be surprised at how your network spreads out with a little effort. Record your findings.

1. Person _____

   Relationship to you _____

   Information/People to contact/Other resources

   a. _____

   b. _____

   c. _____

2. Person _____

   Relationship to you _____

   Information/People to contact/Other resources

   a. _____

   b. _____

   c. _____

3. Person _____

   Relationship to you _____

   Information/People to contact/Other resources

   a. _____

   b. _____

   c. _____

Alex Estrella, a high school student in Arizona, makes his case for networking: "I feel that the best way to get contacts is to be yourself. I get contacts by finding out something personal about people and remembering their names. When I meet business people, I will stay and talk to them and give them my business. They help me out in return and give me discounts." And jobs, too, maybe, down the road!

Job Applications

At this point in your life, most of the jobs you'll apply for don't require résumés or cover letters. You'll simply need to fill out an application. If your application is approved, someone will call you in for an interview. I've included a sample application for you to fill out just for practice. Most applications follow the same format.

Applications

What is important when you are filling out an application?

Be legible. Having the most impressive application in the history of the world won't do you any good if no one can read it. Be honest with yourself. If your writing is terrible, type the application. If you can print neatly, filling it in by hand will do.

Be complete. Make sure you read the instructions carefully and answer all required questions thoroughly. If a question does not apply to you, write "N/A" for "not applicable." Don't hesitate to get help if you don't know some numbers or facts.

Be honest. Any lie that you put on a job application can come back to haunt you. State your age correctly. If you are too young to apply for a certain job, there is probably a reason you shouldn't do it. Employees at certain jobs have to exceed an age limit because of the responsibilities they take on. Legal liability for the employer may come into play. A restaurant, for example, can get fined or even closed if it allows a minor to serve alcohol.

Be honest and clear also about your experience and references. You don't want to be hired to do something that you don't know how to do, or to find out that your interviewer has called an unreliable reference. People will often call references to check up on you, because their business success depends on employee quality, and they want to be sure that your level of experience and competence is what you say it is and will benefit the company. If you have no related experience or no job experience at all, be up front about that, too. We all have to start somewhere. If prospective employers see that you are smart and willing to learn, they may give you a chance—your positive attitude may be worth more to them than experience.

Sample Application for Employment

APPLICATION FOR EMPLOYMENT
(PRE-EMPLOYMENT QUESTIONAIRE)   (AN EQUAL OPPORTUNITY EMPLOYER)

Personal Information

Date _____

Name _____ Soc. Sec. # _____
     Last   First   Middle

Present Address _____
     Street   City   State

Permanent Address _____
     Street   City   State

Phone No. _____ Are You 18 Years Or Older ☐ Yes   ☐ No

SPECIAL QUESTIONS
Do not answer **any** of the questions in this framed area unless the employer has **checked** a **box** **preceding** a question, thereby indicating that the information is required for a bona fide occupational qualification, or dictated by national security laws, or is needed for other legally permissible reasons.

☐ Height _____ feet _____ inches   ☐ Citizen of U.S. Yes _____ No _____

☐ Weight _____ lbs.   ☐ Date of Birth* _____

☐ What Foreign Languages do you speak fluently? _____ Read _____ Write _____

☐ _____

*The Age Discrimination in Employment Act of 1967 prohibits discrimination on the basis of age with respect to individuals who are at least 40 but less than 70 years of age.

EMPLOYMENT DESIRED

Position _____   Date You Can Start _____   Salary Desired _____

Are You Employed Now? _____ If So May We Inquire Of Your Present Employer? _____

Ever Applied To This Company Before? _____ Where? _____ When? _____

EDUCATION	Name and Location of School	*No. of Years Attended	*Did You Graduate?	Subjects Studied
Grammar School				
High School				
College				
Trade, Business or Correspondence School				

*The Age Discrimination in Employment Act of 1967 prohibits discrimination on the basis of age with respect to individuals who are at least 40 but less than 70 years of age.

GENERAL

Subject of Special Study or Research Work _____

U.S. Military or Naval Service_____

Present Membership in National Guard or Reserves_____

QUIKCO   77 105   (continued on other side)

Last

First

Middle

FORMER EMPLOYERS (List below last four employers, starting with last one first).

Date Month & Year	Name and Address of Employer	Salary	Position	Reason for Leaving
From				
To				
From				
To				
From				
To				
From				
To				

REFERENCES: Give the names of three persons not related to you, whom you have known at least one year.

	Name	Address	Business	Years Acquainted
1				
2				
3				

PHYSICAL RECORD

Do you have any physical limitations that preclude you from performing any work for which you are being considered? ☐ Yes ☐ No

Please Describe _____

In Case Of Emergency Notify _____

Name   Address   Phone No

"I certify that the facts contained in this application are true and complete to the best of my knowledge and understand that, if employed, falsified statements on this application shall be grounds for dismissal.

I authorize investigation of all statements contained herein and the references listed above to give you any and all information concerning my previous employment and any pertinent information they may have, personal or otherwise, and release all parties from all liability for any damage that may result from furnishing same to you.

I understand and agree that, if hired, my employment is for no definite period and may, regardless of the date of payment of my wages and salary, be terminated at any time without prior notice."

Date _____ Signature _____

Do Not Write Below This Line

_____ Date _____

_____

_____

Hired: ☐ Yes ☐ No _____ Position _____ Dept. _____

Salary/Wage _____ Date reporting to work _____

Approved: 1. _____ 2. _____ 3. _____

       Employment Manager   Dept. Head   General Manager

77 105

Résumés

A few jobs require a résumé. Often these are jobs that demand more specific skills and a stronger commitment, the kinds you will apply to if you are looking to work full-time after high school. Writing a résumé is an exercise in trying to summarize yourself in one page—not an easy task. But the main purpose of the résumé is to get you in the door, not to get you the job—you do that in person if you get the interview. Résumés should be neat, clean, concise, and impressive enough to make a prospective employer want to meet you and find out who is behind the activities and facts listed on the page. What elements make up a good résumé?

1. **Personal Information**

   At the top of the page you should have your full legal name, current address, and phone number (you may also want to list your social security number).

2. **Job Objective**

   This is a statement that tells what you are seeking in a job—what kind of position, responsibility, and/or skill. Be brief—one sentence is plenty.

3. **Work Experience**

   List the jobs that you have held and your job description/responsibilities for each, in chronological order with the most recent job first and the earliest job last. For each entry, name the company, the dates you worked there, your title if you had one, and what you did.

4. **Education**

   List your high school (don't go any earlier) and the number of years that you have been in attendance there. If you have studied in any special summer programs, list those, too, as long as they are of an academic nature. If you are graduating this year, you can mention the date you'll graduate. If you have made the honor roll, don't forget to include that! And if you have already been accepted into a college, put that in, as well as scholarships you may have won in the process.

5. **Activities/Honors**

List any teams, clubs, or organizations you belong to, and if you are an officer of any kind with a group (team captain, vice president, social chairman, etc.). Honors are any awards that you have won while in high school. Honors can be winning a poetry contest, a high class ranking, winning a spot on an all-country sports team, or an award for outstanding service to your school or community. Don't be shy. Take credit for your accomplishments.

6. **References**

Type the phrase "Personal references available upon request" at the bottom of your résumé. If a prospective employer asks about your references, provide the information at that time (names, phone numbers, addresses, and the relation each reference has to you—friend, father, former boss, etc.). Take with you to any interview a sheet of paper with that information typed neatly on it, so that it is all ready for you to give someone if you need to.

Always type your résumé. Unlike a job application, even if your handwriting is beautiful, a handwritten résumé is not acceptable. Type it on a typewriter, using good-quality paper, or key it into a computer and print it out. If you are using a computer, be sure that the printer paper is good and that the printer is letter-quality. Dot-matrix printing can be difficult to read.

Start by listing everything you want to include, then be selective and narrow it down so that it isn't longer than one page—employers have only so much time and prefer résumés to be short and to the point. If your résumé is just a few lines too long, you may be able to keep all of your information on it by extending the bottom margin a tad or reducing the size of the type or font. This may get you that extra space you need. Be sure that you don't make the type so small as to be illegible, though! Better to have a shorter, readable résumé than a long one that makes the reader's eyes tired. If you have so much information that you have to delete some, decide carefully which parts are the least useful. Delete some of the earliest entries or entries that have no relation to the job you're applying for.

If your résumé seems too short, ask someone you know for help—maybe you have forgotten a job, an activity, or an honor. If you don't have a lot of specific job experience, you can create a skill-based résumé that focuses on your skills, no matter where you got them, rather than job experience. Think about tasks you have performed for your family or friends. If you have cared for children, helped parents or relatives at work, learned some computer skills, done yard work in the neighborhood, sold items door to door, or done anything else that seems marketable, you can put it on a résumé. Refer to the sample for a look at how it can be done.

Sample Résumé

AMIE BONILLA
575 Shayna Lane, #3A
Arlington, VA 22203
703/555-8055

JOB OBJECTIVE: A position that utilizes and develops my computer skills

SKILLS: Microsoft Word 6.0; beginning Lotus 1-2-3; keyboarding, 50 wpm; dBase IV

WORK EXPERIENCE:

CompUSA, Arlington, Virginia
Clerk, part-time, November 1994–present
—Assist customers on the sales floor
—Restock depleted items
—Operate register
—Take customer phone orders

Zoe Publishing, Alexandria, Virginia
Intern, June through August 1994
—Entered inventory and sales data into computer system
—Keyboarded and printed correspondence using Microsoft Word
—Updated database and eliminated out-of-date items

TGIFriday's Restaurant, Arlington, Virginia
Server, September 1993–January 1994
—Took orders and served customers in designated station
—Assisted in coordinating employee scheduling

EDUCATION:

Lakewood High School, Arlington, Virginia
Junior; anticipated graduation June 1996

ACTIVITIES / HONORS:

Lakewood High School, Arlington, Virginia
  Honor Roll, all quarters to present
  Student Council representative for junior class
  Vice president, Computer Club
  Varsity soccer, co-captain

PERSONAL REFERENCES AVAILABLE UPON REQUEST

Sample Skill-based Résumé

AMIE BONILLA
575 Shayna Lane, #3A
Arlington, VA 22203
703/555-8055

JOB OBJECTIVE: A position that utilizes and develops my computer skills

SKILLS:

Technology—Microsoft Word 6.0; beginning Lotus 1-2-3; dBase IV; keyboarding, 50 wpm

Information processing—Entered inventory and sales data into database; updated database items (books, sales, stock); processed customer orders

Organization—Kept files and made photocopies; kept track of items in stock; helped to coordinate restaurant employee schedules

Communication—Handled telephone calls, both incoming and outgoing; reported to managers in both retail and restaurant settings; dealt with retail customers; communicated with other students and teachers as a member of the student council

WORK EXPERIENCE:

CompUSA, Arlington, Virginia. **Clerk**, November 1994–present

Zoe Publishing, Alexandria, Virginia. **Intern**, June through August 1994

TGIFriday's Restaurant, Arlington, Virginia. **Server**, September 1993– January 1994

EDUCATION:

Lakewood High School, Arlington, VA
Current junior; anticipated graduation June 1996
Honor Roll, all quarters to present
Student Council representative for junior class
Vice president, Computer Club
Co-captain, Varsity soccer

PERSONAL REFERENCES AVAILABLE UPON REQUEST

Cover Letters

Include a cover letter with any résumé. A cover letter is your opportunity to be more personal and personable. Résumés are factual and straightforward, and they are not specifically addressed to any one person, even though the objective may be tailored to a certain kind of job. In the cover letter, you can address the person directly and help them get to know you better.

Type your cover letter, and remember to sign it in your own handwriting. Use a nice sheet of paper or stationery. Make it brief—two or three short paragraphs and a closing are plenty. You don't want to take up the reader's time; you just want to spark enough interest to get yourself an interview. The sample will give you an idea of a workable format.

In your first paragraph, talk about the job you want and how you found out about it (a contact, a newspaper listing, etc.). In the second paragraph, restate in a conversational tone the facts in your résumé that you most want the reader to notice. This calls the important facts to the person's attention even before they get to the résumé and interests them in the rest of the résumé. Then briefly tell this prospective employer why it is smart to hire you—talk about the qualifications you have that would make you an ideal employee. In the last paragraph, politely request an interview, state that you will contact them if you don't hear anything within a few weeks, and thank them for their attention.

If you don't get the call, don't immediately take it personally and feel that you are unworthy. Any number of things could have happened. Maybe your letter arrived after people had already been interviewed, and the employer did not have time to interview any more candidates. Maybe someone in the company got a friend or relative in for an early interview and that person was hired. Sometimes things get lost in the mail, or on someone's messy desk. Rather than making yourself miserable, just call and find out what happened with your application. Give your name and ask if the materials were received, if the job has been filled, and if your application was considered. If the situation was out of your control, so be it.

Interviews

If and when you are called for an interview, prepare ahead of time to assure yourself a successful meeting. First of all, write the date and time of the interview where you will see it—in a daily calendar, on a

Sample Cover Letter

575 Shayna Lane, #3A
Arlington, VA 22203
June 2, 1995

Mr. Gary Kline
ABS Enterprises
255 Edgemont Drive, Suite #208
Arlington, VA 22201

Dear Mr. Kline:

I am junior at Lakewood High School, where I am currently taking advanced computer science. I found out about your job opening from my computer teacher, Mr. Mike Siegert.

I am interested in applying to work at ABS Enterprises for two reasons. One, my skills seem to be in line with what you require for the assistant position. I have studied basic programming for two years, I am learning Lotus 1-2-3, and I have a working knowledge of Microsoft Word from my experience last summer as an intern with Zoe Publishing. Also, I am employed part-time at CompUSA on the floor, where I assist customers. Two, I intend to make computers my career and want to take every opportunity to expand my knowledge.

Enclosed is my résumé, which details my work experience and my education. If you would like to interview me in person, I can be reached at 703/555-8055. If I don't hear from you by June 19, I will call you. Thank you for your kind consideration, and I look forward to hearing from you soon.

Sincerely,

Amie Bonilla

Enclosure

scheduling page in your notebook, or posted somewhere in your home. Tell people in your household about it so they can remind you. Forgetting an interview date or being late doesn't say good things about you to your prospective boss. If you can't get it together to show up for your interview, how prompt and efficient will you be on the job? Also make sure you know the exact address where you need to go and how to get there. Ask for directions or for public transportation information. Estimate your travel time and give yourself a buffer zone of extra time in case you run into traffic, get lost, or have trouble getting the bus or train.

When you note your interview date and time, also write the name and number of your contact. Should anything happen—a family problem, a medical emergency, a broken-down subway train, a flat tire—call the contact the instant you know you won't be able to make it. Apologize for the problem, explain what is going on, and ask if you can reschedule. It's normal to feel so bad about the mishap that you would rather avoid the embarrassment of calling. But your promptness and honesty will be appreciated and you'll have spared them the wait.

Spend some time on your appearance when you interview. Heather Pollack almost suffered from a clothing mistake: "I showed up for my interview at the movie theater dressed in sloppy jeans and a flannel T-shirt and brought a friend with me! Both of these spell disaster in a job interview. The manager said later that under normal circumstances she never would have hired me because of the way I hadn't even bothered to clean up, but my friend who worked there recommended me so highly that she gave me a chance."

In order to avoid taking chances like this, find something neat, clean, and neutral to wear—no jeans or beat-up sneakers, no flashy or revealing clothing. For an office job, you should dress in a businesslike manner—usually a skirt or a dress for a woman, and a jacket, tie, and nice shoes for a man. For less formal jobs, you should still dress nicely. Just use your common sense. A neat appearance shows that you take responsibility, you respect the interviewer and the job, and you know how to get along in the world. Don't let your appearance cheat you out of a job where you would be happy and perform well.

When you arrive at the interview, be early and have a pen and paper with you to take notes during the conversation if you need to. You might even have notes you made beforehand about questions you want to ask. You might be nervous—don't worry! Shake hands with the interviewer, make eye contact, and go in for your chat. You'll be talking anywhere from ten minutes to half an hour—it varies according to the person and the job.

What are the most important things to remember while interviewing?

1. Relax and be yourself. This is the chance your interviewer has to really get to know you. If you are so nervous that your true personality doesn't emerge, you are doing yourself a disservice. Let your uniqueness shine through in a confident but not overly comfortable way. Use what you know about basic etiquette—don't put down other people you have worked with, avoid any inappropriate language, and stay attentive. Let the best of you emerge.

2. Listen. An interview is a two-way street! As you will be telling about yourself, your interviewer will tell you about the company, the job, and what kind of person is being sought for the position. You both have to make a decision. You don't have to take a job that you don't think you will like, even if you are offered the position. Make sure this is really the right place for you.

Listening is also crucial because you want to answer the interviewer's questions accurately and completely. Sometimes people get so nervous that they don't hear questions well and they answer incompletely or not at all. Don't fall into that trap! Let the interviewer set the pace. Listen carefully to the questions and answer them completely. Here are some questions you may hear in an interview. I left space so that you can write down some practice answers.

1. Why should we hire you? (Talk about your skills and good qualities.)

_____

_____

_____

2. Tell me about yourself. (Talk about your interests and how they relate to this job.)

_____

_____

_____

3. Talk about your education. (Describe your education so far and emphasize anything that applies to the job.)

_____

_____

_____

4. What experience has prepared you for this job? (Talk about experiences from other jobs as well as from life.)

_____

_____

_____

5. What are your hobbies/favorite activities? (Talk about ones that relate to the job as well as ones that show valuable qualities such as responsibility, dedication, promptness.)

_____

_____

_____

6. What do you consider your greatest talent or accomplishment? (Talk about what you really want them to remember about you.)

_____

_____

_____

7. How have you overcome difficulty in your life? (Discuss something tough that you worked through—it will show your strength and ingenuity.)

_____

_____

_____

8. How would your friends describe you? (A chance to name your best qualities.)

_____

_____

_____

You certainly won't hear *all* of these questions just as they are written here. Often you will hear versions of them more specific to the job at hand. But it's good to rehearse your responses to them, anyway. Just be sure to listen carefully and answer what is asked, instead of delivering a canned response that you have memorized before coming in.

3. Question. You have as much right to ask questions as they do. Think about what you want to know about the job. You might ask: Is this job part-time or full-time? What is the schedule? What is the salary? How flexible is the schedule? How can I advance? Are there any benefits (health insurance, workmen's compensation, travel allowances, discounts, etc.)? Are there any dress or skill requirements?

Don't bombard the interviewer with your questions right away. You will generally have to answer questions first. At one point you may hear, "Do you have any questions for me?" Or it may just be that there comes a point in the interview where you feel it is appropriate to start making your inquiries. Either way, be curious but not insistent. Just ask the questions that you need to be informed about your choice.

Sometimes you will know the outcome right away, such as when I interviewed for the hostess job and was offered the job on the spot. Usually the interviewer thanks you for your time and says you will receive a call. Say your thank-yous in return, and go do something relaxing if you can! Don't dwell on what happened, whether you think it went well or not. Now you have to wait and see. Your interviewer will evaluate you on your congeniality, professionalism, adaptability, responsibility, and accomplishments and potential.

Melissa Rekas was surprised by the outcome of a job interview. "My mom had seen a notice at the library that they were looking for help at $5.10 an hour, so I applied. After two weeks I figured I wouldn't get an interview, but then a week after that they called me. I wore a nice dress and walked in to see two ladies, one with a clipboard who wrote a lot, the other who seemed to conduct most of the interview. They were stiff and strict, and they didn't smile much. They made me nervous, but I tried to smile and to be as nice and friendly as I could.

"They asked me why I wanted the job, why I would be good for it, and what I would do in certain situations, like if I was asked a question that I didn't know. Then they had me do a typing test and an exercise where I had to put catalogue cards in alphabetical order. When I left I didn't feel too good about the whole thing, since they were so serious. I had been in there about ten or fifteen minutes. After a week or so, again I figured I didn't get the job; but at the very end of the period of time they had indicated when they told me when they would contact me, they called and offered me the job. So my advice is to be as friendly as you can no matter what people do, and not to worry about the outcome, because you never know."

Make sure that no matter how you feel about the interview and whether you actually want the job or not, you send a thank-you note to the person who interviewed you. Thank them for their time, and if you do still want the job, mention that you are still interested. Indicate that you will call if you do not hear from the person by a certain date. That way you will have an answer, whether they call you or not, and you can foresee an end to that annoying waiting time.

College Applications and Interviews

College applications, like job applications, request your personal data and references. But they also require you to submit your academic record and your scores on tests like the SAT, ACT, or Advanced Placement exams, and they may ask for a written essay. Much more than when applying for a job, your grades and your test scores make a difference, because not all colleges even have interviews—the larger ones, especially, have no time to interview all of their candidates, and make choices based solely on applications.

Sample Thank-You Note

575 Shayna Lane, #3A
Arlington, VA 22203
June 23, 1995

Mr. Gary Kline
ABS Enterprises
255 Edgemont Drive, Suite #208
Arlington, VA 22201

Dear Mr. Kline:

Thank you for your time yesterday. I enjoyed meeting you and appreciate your continuing to consider me for the position of
assistant during the summer. Your company is very impressive, and
I feel excited about the prospect of working there. I also believe that
my skills would meet your needs well.

I look forward to hearing from you soon.

Sincerely,

Amie Bonilla

SAT tests inspire fear in many high school students, because colleges seem to pay a lot of attention to them when choosing whom to accept. Some students would agree with Melville, New York, native Paul Youkilis's feelings. "In high school, I was a math idiot. I could never do math problems. When I had to take the SAT, it was horrible because it forced me to study for something which I felt had no significant meaning. I think this test isn't about how smart you are or how many books you have read or math problems you have done; it's about how much money your parents have to spend on tutors. I got an 870 on the PSAT before tutors, and then on the SAT I got a 1010, all due to tutors. I was so nervous and stressed out, and I felt that my life depended on this test. Colleges look at the SAT as an indicator of your brain power, and I feel that this is wrong. The whole experience was horrible for me!"

Yes, SATs are important, but they aren't the only thing that colleges look at. Still, you should give your all when you take the test—better safe than sorry. There are books available that can help you prepare by introducing you to the kinds of question you will have to answer and by giving you opportunities to take practice tests. Also, you can take a course that will prepare you for the SAT from a testing service like Stanley Kaplan or the Princeton Review. Such classes will meet regularly for a number of weeks and will cost some money—how much will depend on the kind of test you are training to take. You can even find private tutors to help you prepare, perhaps through one of the testing services just mentioned, or even through your school—check with your guidance counselor.

On your application, be honest about all the facts and figures. Colleges can check your information with your high school or the testing service that gave you any standardized tests. If you are required to write an essay, it gives you a better chance to paint a detailed picture of who you are and what you can do. Write about something that means a lot to you, whether you have free rein to choose your subject or have to limit your topic to something chosen for you. The stronger you feel about your subject, the more you will have to say, and the better you will say it.

Mira Lowenthal, a native of Seattle, Washington, and now a college graduate, had success with her college application essay. "I was very serious about dance at the time, and I wrote about the piece I most loved to perform—a series of short dances choreographed to a group of classical pieces for piano. I didn't make general comments about who I am—I just talked in detail about how I felt about the piece, my role in it, the other dancers, and the legacy of the choreographer and of our teacher, who was his student; the picture of 'the real me' emerged through all of that.

"I am now on a committee that reviews essays written by students applying for the same scholarship I had in college. The introduction to the essay tells the student to write something that helps the reader to learn about him or her—values, experiences, and interests—and suggests describing an influential person or event, future goals, or anything else that would help the reader to know the student. Without fail, the best essays tell a specific story or discuss a specific feeling. The not-so-good ones say things like 'Such-and-such shows my character and my values.' Don't *tell* the reader what your values and character points are—*show* them, through an account of something close to your heart. Also, stick to one subject or story—if it's something you're passionate about, you'll have plenty to say."

If you do go in to interview, the best way you can shine is just to be yourself and relax. The interviewer will be looking for a person who will add something special and live up to the standards that the school has set for itself. You don't have to sell them on your specific skills or experience as you do in a job interview. You want to show that you would be a positive force in the school environment and that you have goals you think studying at this school will help you fulfill. Talk about your interests, your ambitions, what you want to study and why, and why you are interested in this particular school. It probably will be much more of a casual conversation than a job interview. However, you still need to dress neatly, cleanly, and neutrally. Call attention to yourself, not your appearance.

Success and Failure

Sometimes you win, and it's the best, and sometimes you lose, and you're miserable. Everyone gets some of both in life, although when you're losing, it looks as if everyone else in the world is winning (it's not true, it just looks that way). But life goes on—success and failure are only brief flashes on the road of everyday living. A failure eventually leads to another try, and a success leads to having to get back to work in the quest to achieve new goals.

When you have a big success, you deserve to have some fun with family or friends, a night out or a nice dinner or whatever you like, to enjoy your victory. But remember that your success has only opened a door, and now you have to prepare yourself to face what lies beyond the door. You will have to work hard at your job to live up to what your supervisor thought of you in the interview, or you will have to work hard at college to make the most of the money and time you are putting toward your education. Success isn't the top of the mountain; it's getting in the gate at the bottom to let you start climbing. Here's how James Morris defines success: "Success is having a satisfying career. By success I also mean being someone who helps people and the community. It's no good to make it and leave your people behind—you need to be there for them."

When you fail or suffer a disappointment, do something nice for yourself to make you feel better. Go out for ice cream, spend an evening being lazy, go out with friends, whatever helps. "I always used to stay in on a Saturday night if I was miserable over something," says Sarah Lyman Kravits. "I'd make a huge bowl of popcorn, pop a Tab, and watch *The Love Boat* and *Fantasy Island* and whatever else as late as I could until my parents made me go to bed. It made it almost cozy to be in a rotten mood, and I always felt better the next day." Then pick yourself up and try again. Apply for a different job, at the same company or elsewhere. Apply to a different college. Take some college courses locally and then apply again to the same college when you feel as if you have more education under your belt. Take the SAT again to raise your scores. If the job or the college is truly what you want, reassess your priorities and find a way to get there.

Sometimes you will not achieve immediate success. Garth Kravits got into college, but on certain conditions. "My grades weren't too good because I hadn't applied myself, so my application was borderline. They said I could enter in the fall only if I took a special summer school program. I decided to do it, because at the time I thought college was the right place for me. When I went to summer school, I was bored with the classes because they were too easy. I discovered that the program was more suited to people who needed to improve their skills than to people like me who had just goofed off. I felt like I wasted my time. Later, I decided that college wasn't my route to success, and I found happiness singing with a band and working as a grill chef in a local restaurant." Garth had to make his way through a few different attempts and failures before he found a path that brought him success—and what he learned on the way helped guide him in the right direction.

Failure is a strong, universal fear among high school students. I heard it again and again like a chorus when I talked to them. "My greatest fear is failure. I am disappointed when I have not accomplished what I want to do," said Sandra McCullough; James Morris revealed that "my greatest fear is that I won't make it in life—that I won't be a

success." "I didn't have problems until junior year," says Jeffrey Hoffman, a recent high school graduate from East Amherst, New York.
"But then I found myself slacking off in my work. My friends were
always going out, and I put them before my studies. I was having fun,
and I didn't realize how I was hurting myself—junior year is important
because it is the year colleges look at and it is when you take your SAT
test. I didn't prepare for the test. Finally I took the SAT and could tell
I didn't do my best. When I received my score, it was a big shock to
me. I failed to do what I expected and had to reevaluate myself. I
wanted to go on to study at a top college, and I realized that my slacking
might prevent me from accomplishing my dream.

"I reorganized my life. I worked hard and was able to say no to
friends and sit down to study. This first SAT failure led to a later score
I was proud of. Even though I had pretty much gotten my work done
before, I realized that sometimes a person needs to work a little harder
than others to stay on a level with them."

Daneka Mocarski hit a roadblock on her way to being a college student. "I had applied to Boston College my senior year, and it was the
only place I wanted to go, although I applied to other schools. First I
was deferred, then I was wait-listed. I figured that I was still in the
running. Then I was wait-listed for a longer time, and finally they
rejected me. I was crushed. I thought I worked my butt off in high
school for nothing, and I didn't work as hard the rest of my senior
year. I received the same grades somehow, and amazingly enough, I
had a lot more fun. I was able to let loose and relax for once. I discovered
during this period that life isn't just about work, but it is about fun,
too, and about being happy.

"Since I relaxed, I was happier than I'd ever been. I learned that
school is what you make of it—it isn't the name or prestige but what
you do with your education. After pondering this for days, I realized
that I was happy to go to another university—Syracuse—instead of
Boston College. If I didn't make it into that school, then I didn't belong
there. Rejection taught me how to be the best me I can be—and if I
wasn't accepted somewhere, then they didn't know what they were
missing."

Your greatest weapon against the fear of failure is your willingness
to try to succeed. It can seem easy just not to try, because then you
don't have to take responsibility for any failure you have. But you
sacrifice the chance to succeed. Success comes only with effort, and if
you fail in your attempt, you can take valuable lessons from your failure
and try again with a better chance.

William Wolfe's father taught him a valuable lesson as he began to apply to colleges. "When I arrived home with my college applications, I sat down and skimmed over them. My father joined me. He asked why I had chosen schools that lacked top-quality educational experiences. I told him that top universities would be academically overwhelming to me and that I'd probably fail. But my father said it doesn't matter if I fail as long as I put my best effort into my work and gain knowledge from my experience, even if the knowledge is that I cannot handle a certain level of work. His words led me to apply to one of the universities I feared, and now here I am at Syracuse. I continue to apply my father's statement to my actions today.

"This quote by Theodore Roosevelt sums it up for my dad and me:

"It is not the critic who counts, not the man who points out how the strong man stumbled, or where the doer of deeds could have done them better. The credit belongs to the man who is actually in the arena; whose face is marred by dust and sweat and blood; who strives valiantly; who errs and comes short again and again; who knows the great enthusiasms, the great devotions, and spends himself in a worthy cause; who, at best, knows in the end the triumph of high achievement; and who, at the worst, if he fails, at least fails while daring greatly, so that his place shall never be with those cold and timid souls who know neither victory nor defeat."

▪ 9 ▪

OPENING DOORS
Joining the Academic and Working Worlds

On January 9, 1961, I walked onto the campus at the University of Georgia to begin registering for classes. Ordinarily, there would not have been anything unusual about such a routine exercise, except, in this instance, the officials at the university had been fighting for two and a half years to keep me out. I was not socially, intellectually, or morally undesirable. I was Black. And no Black student had ever been admitted to the University of Georgia in its 176-year history . . . [The] sense of mission . . . evolved for me out of a natural desire to fulfill a dream I had nurtured from an early age . . . I wanted to be a journalist, a dream that would have been, if not unthinkable, at least undoable in the South of my early years. But no one ever told me not to dream, and when the time came to act on that dream, I would not let anything stand in the way of fulfilling it.

CHARLAYNE HUNTER-GAULT
Journalist/news correspondent
Born 1942

The examples that Charlayne Hunter-Gault's parents and grandparents set taught her early on that the keys to freedom and happiness are a good education and a fulfilling career. Her father was an army chaplain who spoke a number of different languages, and her mother, educated at a high school in Chicago, taught school from time to time and read books voraciously, often one a day. A dictionary was displayed in full view in their house, ready for use. Five-year-old Charlayne started first grade a year early, along with her six-year-old best friend, and ended up advancing to second grade along with the rest of her class. Her first career goal, set while in elementary school, was to be a doctor.

Later, at Turner High School in Atlanta, Charlayne dove into both extracurriculars and academics—she joined clubs, went out for sports teams, and sang with the choir. When her English teacher saw how well she performed, she asked her to help correct papers and prepare materials for other classes. Another teacher who was the adviser for the student newspaper, Mrs. Evans, had her proofread other people's articles and eventually began encouraging her to write her own, even though she was a freshman and the majority of the newspaper staff were upperclassmen. Mrs. Evans was a role model to Charlayne. She had earned a master's degree at the University of Michigan and had worked as a reporter on a local black newspaper. That teacher eventually appointed Charlayne the editor of the school paper, a position she held for two years—she was the first junior to ever become editor.

In her senior year, Charlayne searched for a college that would give her the background in journalism that she wanted. At that time, the black colleges she looked at didn't have journalism departments. She was accepted at Wayne State in Michigan but also decided to apply to the University of Georgia despite its racist attitudes and the fact that no black had ever attended the school. After she attended Wayne State for over a year, she finally got an interview at the University of Georgia. She and her friend Hamilton "Hamp" Holmes, who had also applied, were repeatedly not admitted—because of dorm overcrowding, said the admissions office at the University of Georgia. The two students secured lawyers and went to court to try to prove that the university had denied them entry because of their race, an act that had finally been made illegal.

After a few rounds of legal battles, a federal judge formally admitted them to the University of Georgia. Triumphant but wary, they walked in on their first day surrounded by reporters and taunted by angry white students. Campus officials often had to escort Charlayne to class, and once she and Hamp were suspended for their own safety after rioting became threatening. But they pressed on and graduated with distinction. During her time there, Charlayne nurtured her dream of a journalism career by writing articles about her experience at the University of Georgia for interested publications—among them *The Urbanite*, a New York–based black magazine, and the *Inquirer*, an Atlanta newspaper that focused on the civil rights movement. After her first full year, she won a summer internship at the previously all-white *Louisville Times*.

Charlayne took the education she had fought so long and so hard for and put it to work achieving her dream. Working her way up through the ranks of journalistic writing and television, she now holds an esteemed position as correspondent for PBS's nationally broadcast *MacNeil/Lehrer NewsHour*. She pursued all the avenues open to her and even some that weren't so open. She took advantage of every possible opportunity to learn, whether through school or work, and built upon those opportunities the life she had long wanted for herself. You, too, have these opportunities—maybe even more so today, thanks to people like Charlayne Hunter-Gault, who fought to open doors for herself and for everyone.

When you have a job or the invitation to attend a college, it's a new beginning. You have spent time figuring yourself out, using your resources, going for your goals, presenting yourself well, and following up. Now you have a new chance to move ahead on the road to the life that you want to make for yourself. Don't wait for things to come to you—go out and get them! Instead of waiting around for your life to happen to you, make it happen yourself.

Making the Transition

Whatever your path out of high school, you will have a lot to learn, no matter how prepared you feel. You probably were hired for your job because your interviewer believes you have what it takes to do the work required, or you were accepted at a college because you seem to have the intelligence and work ethic to succeed. Still, those skills are just the tip of the iceberg. You are entering a completely new world.

The first step, and often a difficult one, is that choice between work and further schooling. If you have a good idea of your chosen career, then you can begin to plan while still a high school student. You will know in your junior year if you want to visit colleges, trade schools, or companies. You can more efficiently choose electives that may help you achieve your goals. You will have a head start. The caretakers in your life won't necessarily be taking care of you forever! Pretty soon you will be taking care of yourself, so now is a good time to start taking that kind of responsibility for your life.

Recently the U.S. government has officially recognized the need for a stronger emphasis on career education and information in the nation's high schools. This has resulted in the passing of the School-to-Work legislation, which orders schools to begin integrating more career education into the curriculum. This legislation may trickle down to you in a number of ways, depending on your individual school. You may have already experienced some of the following.

- *Career centers* with a variety of services available to students, some required, some optional

- A *requirement* that high school juniors decide on a career path and begin to research it
- *Computerized "Interest Surveys,"* such as the one offered by the "Choices" computer, which ask a variety of personal questions and then suggest possible career paths based on the answers
- *School-sponsored opportunities* to talk to people about their careers
- *Chances to intern,* work part-time, or "shadow" an employee for a day to find out more about a specific career
- *Compiling a personal folder or "portfolio"* with all information pertaining to career planning—interest surveys, listings of education/training/ work experience/volunteer experience, résumé, letters of recommendation, certificates and/or awards, future goals, personal interests

Freshmen or sophomores might feel funny thinking this far ahead, but *it is never too early for career exploration.* You've already started by just reading this book and thinking about yourself, your dreams, and your talents. You can always change your mind! The important thing is to *have a direction,* any direction. A goal-directed person is on the move to somewhere, anywhere, and that motion is crucial. Once you are in motion, you have the power to focus your energy, and aim where you decide you want to be. You can change directions only if you have a direction to start with.

Workplace

Working brings you a whole new set of responsibilities, especially if you are working full-time after graduating from high school. Instead of going to school because you have to, following the directives of teachers and parents, you are working for someone else who depends on you and you receive money in exchange for your work. If you ever missed school, you affected only yourself. As a working person, if you blow off work, you take the chance of hurting the business for which you work as well as the people who work with you. In taking on your particular end of the bargain, you are responsible for keeping the whole operation running. Every person's job is an important part of the whole.

You also may find that you represent something different to people than you do as a student in school. "When I worked in a movie theater during my senior year, I learned that it is difficult to work in a service industry," says Gwenan Wilbur. "You don't really exist when you work behind a counter selling food. No matter how courteous you are to people, they see you as a dispenser of material items they want quickly.

It was very demoralizing." Jim Lindsey had a similar experience working in a fast-food restaurant: "I learned that even though you worked hard, the customers didn't really respect you very much. That was irritating." It can be hard to adjust to feeling like less of a person around customers.

"But at least I had money of my own," says Gwenan. "Sometimes I think the reason my parents didn't push me to get a job sooner was because they wanted me to feel dependent on them. Having my own money made me more in control of my life."

Since you have more responsibility as a working person, you need to adhere to the system of operation that your business uses. There are hundreds of restaurants, or law firms, or retail clothing stores, or accounting firms that generally perform the same functions. But each one in a given category has its own particular way of working. Factors include:

- The work schedule
- The hierarchy—people to whom you report, and those who report to you
- The priorities—the items that always need to be addressed first
- The way in which employees move up in the ranks
- The way goals are set and duties delegated
- The values and ideals of the company

Give yourself a chance to get used to the new environment. You won't do everything right at first. Here, as well as in so many other situations, you will learn from your mistakes. Your boss or supervisor will probably give you a basic outline of how things work, and it's important to take it all in. But your supervisors cannot possibly think of, or describe to you, every different situation that you will encounter. Part of the reason why employers like to hire smart people is that they want employees who can handle unusual situations wisely when they arise. You need to be able to think on your feet and find solutions quickly when something takes you by surprise.

You can learn a lot from the people you work with who have been there for a while. Be open to getting to know them, and never be afraid to ask for their help when you are confused. They used to be where you are, and they probably had a lot of the same questions you have and made mistakes similar to those that you may make. When Nicole Caplan worked for her mom, she gained all kinds of knowledge, both general and specific, about the business. "My choice to work with my mother had a dramatic influence on me. For the first time, I was part of a collaborative team that created a foundation for the future of a business. I had no experience but was forced to learn fast and use ingenuity, common sense, and research tactics—qualities I never knew I had. I learned to be resourceful in business situations and negotiations. I also learned all about being an executive recruiter in the pharmaceutical industry (my mom's line of work)."

College

My first semester of college was a rough time of adjustment. I attended a state university with 35,000 students and I lived in a large dorm with several hundred women. My roommate was one of my best friends in high school, but we did a role reversal. In high school she was the studious one who seldom went out late to play while I was always up for going out on both weekdays and weekends. Now she was taking advantage of her new college freedom while I was becoming aware of my college responsibilities and didn't want to blow my chance to excel. Our different goals put a strain on our relationship, and we grew apart.

I also joined a sorority. Although I hadn't planned to do it, my mom encouraged me and I finally gave it a try. I'm glad I did, because I learned a lot about dealing with all kinds of people in very close quarters—the good, the bad, and the ugly. I also made some friends who are still my best friends to this day.

Finally, I felt a lot of pressure to succeed in college. I knew I had not applied myself during high school, and this was my one big opportunity to learn all I could. I didn't want to screw up. I definitely had to take time to adjust to working hard and giving up some of my social time for the purpose of keeping up with my studies. I may not have been to as many parties or had as large a group of friends, but the work I accomplished made up for it, and the friends who stuck with me even when I had to study were the ones who were really worth my time and energy.

College takes some adjustment, especially if you are living away from home. You may have to share a room for the first time in your life— suddenly, when you want certain music on or want to go to sleep early or stay up late with the lights on, your desires affect someone else, too, and sometimes clash with what the other person wants or needs. You may share a common space—a hall or living room—with anywhere from five to forty other people. Living in close quarters takes a lot of compromise and cooperation.

You are also going to be much more responsible for yourself—what time you get up and when you go to bed, how much you sleep, what and when you eat, what you wear, how much work you do, how much you play. No one is there to tell you what to do, and you may react by behaving in the exact opposite way to the way you did when your parents were responsible for you, as both my roommate and I did. More may be at stake in how well you do in your studies. Your college academic record will carry more weight in the working world than your high school record. Therefore, a successful college career can help you find the work you want, while a so-so record could hamper you.

Also, for those of you who attended public high school, college is different because you're paying for it! It doesn't make sense to spend all that money if you are going to waste your time and ignore your work. Even if you are on scholarship, someone is laying out money for your education. You may feel more responsibility because of that fact. It contributed to Garth Kravits's decision to leave: "I felt guilty that I was on scholarship and was spending all of my time partying instead of studying. When I left, I told them that they should give the scholarship to someone who would really use it and appreciate it. College just wasn't the place for me." The truth is, you could get a job, make money, and have fun in your off hours instead of spending money on classes that you would rather not attend. That's why it's important to make sure you really want to be in college if you make that choice.

One more adjustment to make in college is to get used to the kind of work, and the amount of work, that it sends your way. You will have more work, and harder work, than you had in high school— although it will also be less boring and more satisfying work, and as you progress past the required classes, it will more often be work that you choose based on your own interests. It won't be impossible, it will just take more time and concentration than it used to. You will have more time, though—at the most you will take five or six classes, and classes generally meet three times a week for fifty minutes each time or twice a week for an hour and a quarter. In high school, your classes meet mostly five times a week for about fifty minutes, and you have six or seven classes on any given day. You will need the extra time that the college schedule gives you—use your scheduling skills to make the most of it.

Even if you make the choice to attend college and begin your studies, keep yourself open to other possibilities. Many students transfer to different schools, either because they haven't made the best choice or because they discover needs that their present schools cannot satisfy. Lisa Ivy, an African American from Chicago who attends a small private college in southern Illinois, decided to go there because she liked the recruiter and because she thought it looked peaceful when she visited. "Now I'm having second thoughts. I grew up in the city, where there's always something going on. Now, once the sun goes down here, there's nothing to do. When I look out my dorm window, all I see is cornfields in the darkness.

"Most of the students are from the farms nearby, and they like country-western music, not rap and contemporary pop, like I do. They even play it in the cafeteria. I am one of very few African Americans, and there aren't any minority organizations here. Everyone is nice, but I miss my home buddies. I feel so isolated! One of my high school teachers told me that this school's focus and location wouldn't work for me, but I had already made up my mind. I really didn't ask for advice, and now I regret that. I wish I had included more people in my decision about college, and that I had listened more to that teacher."

Even as it presents challenges, college can be a time of amazingly positive change, especially for people who may have had a tough time in high school. Rex Randall Erickson, now an attorney in San Diego, tells his story: "I grew up in a very small town in Kansas. My high school had 150 people—only forty in my class. I was six-foot-two as a freshman, weighed one hundred pounds, and wore glasses. I was only 130 pounds at graduation. I joined the wrestling team but lost every match my freshman year, tied one my sophomore year, and by my senior year had won a total of only four. I finished dead last in the only varsity cross-country race I ran. I was considered a little weird— my younger brother's friends called me 'freak,' and even I realized that I was different from almost everyone else. Individuality isn't a desired trait in a town where it is the custom to beat up anyone new or different who comes to town. I was considered smart and did very well on standardized college admittance exams, but had just-above-average grades. I dated one girl in high school, for a few months during my junior year. When I graduated in May 1984, I was a tall, skinny, near-sighted, nonathletic, weird, eggheaded near virgin (I got lucky with an old friend one drunken night just before graduation).

"I went to the University of Kansas the following August. During my freshman year, I gained fifty pounds, got contact lenses, and started taking karate. Girls began taking an interest in *me*. I met people with a lot stranger ideas than I ever had, and I learned to enjoy my individuality rather than conceal it. As a sophomore, I placed second in fighting and forms at a national karate tournament in Oklahoma City. Since that time, I have gotten a black belt, received undergraduate degrees in political science and psychology, earned a law degree, and passed the California bar on the first attempt. I am now an attorney in a suburb of San Diego and live thirty feet from the ocean with a wonderful woman. I've gone skydiving and backpacked across Europe. I'm in better shape than I've ever been in my life, mentally and physically. I learned that popularity is a function of your environment—once I hung around people with varying thoughts and experiences, I was able to find my niche and make friends.

"I recently went back to my hometown for my ten-year high school reunion. Of forty people, I was one of three who had a postgraduate degree. Most of the people I had wished I was in high school—the popular people, athletes, and super-smart people—had never progressed past the height of their abilities at that time. I wouldn't trade positions with them now for anything. I think maybe they thought their popularity, athleticism, or intelligence in high school would carry them through the rest of their lives. When it didn't, and they entered a bigger world with better athletes and smarter people, they weren't prepared to handle it."

Social Politics

There are politics in every workplace and in every college environment. You have some experience with politics in high school, even though you may never have thought about your group associations in those terms.

SOCIAL POLITICS, noun.
　the often internally conflicting interrelationships among people in a
　group or society

If you have a pretty close-knit group of friends that hang out together, think about how everyone relates to each other. Probably no one specifically organized that structure, assigning roles that each person would play and levels of influence that each would have, but these things seem to form on their own whenever a group gets together. Is someone the leader of your group? Are some the entertainers, some the core group that has the most power to make decisions, and some the semi-outsiders, not completely accepted? All of this falls under the heading of politics, and it doesn't end after high school.

Heather Pollack was the victim of some particularly mean political moves in high school. "I was on the verge of being accepted into the 'popular' crowd—all appearances indicated I was moving in that direction. I had three good friends who were already there. One day at the pool another girl started talking about my friends and called them 'the biggest sluts in the school.' At that time, I didn't say anything because I didn't really know how to react. Then, shortly after that, I found that people from the popular group shunned me. I couldn't understand and was very upset. Finally someone told me that the girl who had slandered my friends had told people I had agreed with her!

"I learned that people don't always tell the truth and that you shouldn't trust everyone automatically. Unfortunately, this girl had set out to destroy my chances of getting in that group, and she succeeded. There are people like that in my line of work now, and you have to watch yourself. There's not much you can do when something like this happens, but I'm convinced that their bad karma will eventually come back and slap them in their faces."

Workplace

Because of the politics of your workplace, not everything will run according to plan! No matter how many rules a company has, human factors can interfere. For example, say you and another person were hired at the same time, and your jobs are similar and new to both of you. You both work hard, come in on time, and progress well. But the boss can promote only one of you this month, and it ends up being the other person. Why?

Well, perhaps the reason is perfectly legitimate. The other person may have special skills, more training, or a more congenial personality on the job. The other person may have more opportunity and willingness to put in overtime hours. Perhaps it's just the luck of the draw, or maybe you just have no idea at all what made the difference. If you've done your best and the other person clearly had an advantage, you cannot ask more of yourself. Just keep working toward your own personal advancement.

On the other hand, politics may have been a factor. Perhaps the other employee is the daughter of one of the boss's friends. Maybe she and the boss have a close relationship. Maybe the employee's family has invested in the company and has influence over how things work. Perhaps the company needs a woman in a higher position and you are a man. You never know what kind of politics may come into play.

Everything that happens in any workplace will not always be fair, and politics is behind that to some extent. But in accepting it as a part of how things work, you can also use it to your advantage. Be sure to treat everyone with respect. Do your work efficiently. Get to know the people with whom you work. Becoming more a part of your workplace in this way will give you a better chance of being on the beneficial side of the political games. If people like you, they are more likely to think of you when rewards or promotions are at stake.

College

College politics begin with the acceptance process; for example, some schools give preference to "legacies" (people who have a parent who attended the college), and some state schools need to admit a certain number of women and minority students to fill quotas set up by state law. Once you get in, the politics revolve around who does well in class, who gets scholarships, who is asked to join honorary societies, or who is given opportunities to do honors work or independent research. Your talent, hard work, and eligibility should be the only factors, but politics skew the chances. Your best bet is to stay on everyone's good side and do your best as much as you can. That way you will give yourself the best possible chance to benefit from the political system rather than being trampled by it.

Racial and cultural differences can come onto the political scene as well, depending on the school you attend; be aware that they can affect your experience. Lisa Ivy sensed negative attitudes at her college from the start. "First, when a few African-American students wanted to include an African dance as part of an annual fund-raising show, the planning committee told the students that they couldn't include it because one of the prospective dancers was in a couple of other acts. But this seemed like an excuse, because many students were in more than one act.

"Also, in my communications class, when we read an essay by Frederick Douglass that talked about how he didn't celebrate the Fourth of July because he didn't feel like a part of the American dream, one student said that if blacks don't want to celebrate the Fourth, they should go back to Africa. I was the only African American in the class, and I wanted to say something but I couldn't get the words out. It's not that everything is awful—people are nice to me here, we joke around and stuff, but the prejudice comes in subtle ways. I have decided to transfer to a different college next year—one that has more of a focus on minority students."

Street Smarts

Originally, being street-smart, or street-wise, meant that you were actually homeless and lived on the street. Being poor, you had to be resourceful. You had to know where you were going to get your next meal or where you were going to be able to find shelter for the night. You had to know how to avoid thieves and rats.

Today, street smarts still mean knowing your way around, but in a somewhat different context. They have become something you need in order to compete in today's world, over and above any education you have. Without street smarts, you won't be able to perform at your full potential, and may not get to perform at all. With them, you will be able to communicate to the world what you can do and how you intend to do it. You will be able to navigate through the pitfalls of the system with as much success as possible.

You can develop two different types of street smarts: general and specific. Being on time, knowing how to ask questions and to whom to direct them, being kind and positive in your attitude, and being responsible are examples of general street smarts. They will allow you to function efficiently on a daily basis. Judith Goodman, now at Syracuse University, learned from the challenge of being the editor of her school yearbook. "I worked on school yearbooks for four years before I became editor, and I didn't know it would be so hard. I had a staff of twenty students and only four of them worked on the yearbook, so that left me with a lot of work. I had learned, though, from my junior-year experience that you need to be strict and can't be friends with everyone. I learned to be responsible and to put everything else aside and get done what needs to be done—and despite the stress, it was one of the best life lessons that I will ever get."

You also need specific street smarts when you begin to narrow down your interests and focus on a potential career goal. Specific street smarts mean knowing the answers to questions like who is important to know in your field, how people dress for success, what kinds of skills and information you should possess, and what course of action (work experience, schooling, apprenticeships, internships, etc.) you should take to reach your goal. You have to become a student of your chosen path and research what it takes to get you where you want to be.

Andrea Smalling of Brooklyn, New York, found a school organization that helped her get a leg up. "I was the treasurer of my high school's chapter of FBLA—Future Business Leaders of America. This club is designed to help students explore the world of business. Through selling food to raise funds, volunteering to help young people, going to business lectures, and competing with other chapters, we learned about the importance of business, leadership, competition, and proper business behavior. Our meetings were in business format, and we wore business attire when we went outside to raise funds from businesspersons or when we engaged in competitions. We also picked up computer and communication skills. My goal is to have a career in business, and this experience gave me a transition from school to work. My communication, leadership, and computer and teamwork skills will stay in my life."

Developing street smarts takes time—in fact, it can extend over a lifetime. I know I learn new things every day about the publishing business, and I have been here for more than ten years, at all kinds of different jobs. Things change all the time, and continual attention to keeping your street smarts honed will help you stay up-to-date. Three key actions will help you develop street smarts.

1. *Listen.* What do your parents, co-workers, fellow students, supervisors say to each other? What actions are praised, what allowed, what condemned, what punished? What is valued? Everything that you hear—conversations, announcements, events, arguments—can add to your information. But be careful not to assume automatically that anything you hear is useful. Use your instincts. Especially when it comes to what you hear about the people in charge, don't take anyone's word as gospel. Find out for yourself by investigating or trying something out. Soak up all the knowledge you can but make sure to tailor it to your situation.

2. *Observe.* How do people behave? How are duties performed, correctly as well as incorrectly? How do people dress? How do they treat one another, and what kinds of treatment are rewarded or punished? What does the environment look like, and what does that say about how things are run?

3. *Ask questions.* There is no greater source of knowledge about the street smarts you'll need to get into your chosen field than the people who have gotten there before you. They've learned from their experiences—or from asking people when *they* were starting out—and many of them will be happy to share their thoughts. You can talk to supervisors or co-workers at your job, teachers or advisers or fellow students at school, your parents, other friends, or other relatives or counselors.

Ask about whatever you cannot deduce from observation or listening. Ask about who has the most power, who needs the most stroking or attention or understanding or time, who is the most difficult to work with and why, and who makes strategic decisions about hiring and firing that could affect you. Ask about details such as dress, how important is adhering to schedule, format and presentation of work that you do, activities that could benefit you, or people that have similar interests to yours.

After you get the answers to your questions, put your street smarts to use. Adapt your behavior, adjust your tone, imitate what you see around you. Be perceptive. In a lot of ways, acquiring basic street smarts is like acquiring a foreign language. Your job is to figure that language out so you can be conversant with someone else—so you can know how they do it. When you can communicate in this way, you will be able to get what you want.

South Orange, New Jersey, native Kathryn Byrnes is putting her street smarts to use in college and anticipates taking advantage of them in the future. "I went on youth group retreats in high school. I dreaded going to the first one, but it turned out to be one of the best weekends of my life, and the next year I became a group leader. Being part of a team and leading a group, I learned how to work cohesively in a group setting and how to understand all aspects of a team—the leader, the gatekeeper who keeps the group together, and the observer, among others. It can take business people years to develop these skills that I learned in high school. With my teamwork and interpersonal skills, I already have a head start on being a good manager."

Workplace

In the workplace, street smarts include information such as how to address people; how to dress; the power hierarchy—who has power over whom; who is receptive to requests for help; how people treat each other; what kinds of things get you noticed and move you up; customs and standards and company values; who has control and who doesn't; how to get control; how important being on time is; how to win and keep a job; and what types of people succeed in your workplace.

College

At college, developing your street smarts might lead you to find information about topics such as who the best professors are; who the nicest professors are; which classes you need to reach your academic goals; which advisers know how to point you in the right direction; the best places to study efficiently; the extracurriculars that go along with your goals; how to manage your finances; where scholarships and fellowships and grants might be available to you; and where to live.

Some of you might be thinking at this point that developing street smarts means conforming to someone else's idea of who you should be and how you should act. You may be thinking that if you dress, act, and plan according to what other people do or tell you to do, you are selling out, compromising your ideals. But your individuality comes from inside, from your goals and ambitions. There's no shame in exploring established paths in order to get where you want to go. If you don't let your pride get in the way, you may find that doing what your street smarts tell you works may save you quite a bit of time and trouble.

Street smarts help you learn about the trade-offs that you are, or are not, willing to make. If you decide that you won't dress any differently for any job, you may be limited in your opportunities. You might think that the trade of some work opportunities for your individual clothing statement is worth it. Or you may discover that it isn't, and then you won't mind so much dressing in the accepted way for your job interview. The more street smarts you develop, the more easily you will be able to make decisions about your future.

Your Rights on the Job or at School

Just as everyone has rights as citizens of this country, everyone also has rights as employees and students.

Treatment

You have a right to be treated with kindness and respect, no matter where you work or study. Abuse comes in many forms—verbal, psychological, emotional, and physical—and in many levels of seriousness. If for any reason you feel you are being mistreated on the job, take the initiative to address the situation with someone. When things are happening that make you feel uncomfortable or mistreated, you have a right to take steps to fix the problem.

Discrimination and preferential treatment happen from time to time. "I was working at a supermarket," explains Nelson Cruz. "The deli man, who was a different race from me, made a sandwich, ate it, and didn't pay, so I did the same—and I got fired." Whether or not either of them should have done what he did, the fact is that one person was fired and one was not punished and they did the same thing.

Deena Mottola had a negative experience at one job. "When I was fourteen, I started working at a pizzeria. It was fun because it was a hangout for high school kids. Sometimes it was frustrating because I was the only girl working there, and the different duties for men and women were rigid. For instance, I wasn't allowed to make pizza. I had to answer the phone and take the orders. The men could go off and socialize and take breaks, and I never could because I had to man the phones. The men never got yelled at, and I always did, even though I was the one keeping everything going and keeping the pizza makers in line. Finally I quit because I felt I was being harassed by the guys. The job taught me that men and women aren't always treated the same at work and that I'm not willing to accept that."

There are a few different paths that you can take if you are unhappy with your job situation.

- *Grin and bear it.* This is not for everyone, or for every situation. But sometimes your job will be so valuable, and the level of annoyance so low, that you feel rocking the boat would do more harm than good. You have to take a hard look at what you want and what you need. For example, if you know you can get another comparable job easily and you can't stand a certain co-worker's style, you might decide it's worth it to quit. But if your job brings in a very necessary paycheck and isn't so replaceable, you might decide that you can live with annoyance in exchange for security. In another case, if you have a serious problem, such as sexual harassment, you might feel that no job is worth dealing with the treatment you receive. Measure out the pros and cons of your situation—write them down so that everything is clear to you—and decide if staying quiet makes sense.
- *Work the problem out with the source of the problem—co-worker or supervisor.* If the problem is a person and you have had a pretty positive and honest relationship with that person up until now, you might want to try to have an honest conversation together. Find a time when you are both free; schedule the talk ahead of time; talk someplace private and relatively free of distraction. If you can express yourself,

you feel that your concerns are heard, and you are able to agree on changes that satisfy you, this is the least painful way to resolve a problem. If you aren't happy with the outcome, move on to another step of action.

- *Consult a superior who has no direct involvement in the situation but who can help you resolve it.* If the previous option doesn't work, if you don't feel comfortable talking with the person causing the problem, or if the problem involves something like conditions or salary, you can go to someone outside the situation. If conditions, money, or a co-worker is causing you stress, go to a supervisor. If a supervisor is the problem, find someone else whose status is equal to or greater than the supervisor's. Schedule a private meeting and talk honestly about what is troubling you. Ideally, the supervisor should be able to exercise enough power to change the situation for the better. This change could involve changes in conditions, a simple conversation with the problem person, a shift in responsibilities for you or someone else, or a request for the problem person or you (or both of you) to leave if you cannot work together.
- *Leave your job.* If you find no relief, you may want to get out of the situation altogether. To save yourself additional trouble and maybe even secure yourself a positive reference for the future, give adequate notice of your leaving (usually two weeks). Inform your supervisor first, before you tell anyone else in the company. When you talk with the supervisor, be as honest as you can about why you are leaving. You have the right to speak up about problems and mistreatment—for the sake of your own sanity as well as for the sake of the company and others there. You might not be the only one who has experienced the problem, and your honesty may help others in the long run. When it comes to others with whom you work, why you're leaving is your business, and you have the right to keep it to yourself, which you may want to do if the problem is personal. You may want to let people know if you feel your problem may affect others and you want to warn them of trouble, but be smart: try to leave on good terms.

Says Sharifah Sams, "I worked for a hospital for mentally ill people. When I started, one of the patients liked me and he followed me everywhere. I was afraid because I've never been in a situation like that. One of the nurses that worked there had to tell him to leave me alone." When things don't feel right, do something about it! Don't do yourself the disservice of staying in a situation that could be damaging to you in any way. You have a right to be content and respected.

Feedback

Whether at work or at school, you have a right to know how you are doing. You may receive a periodic work review from your boss, and your report card performs that service at school. But you may also request more frequent feedback from your supervisor or teacher about how you are doing and if you are on the right track. If you are making mistakes, you deserve to know it early enough to have time to correct them before they get you in real trouble. You can't correct a mistake until you know you have made one, and it is up to your boss or teacher to let you know that you need to fix something that you did wrong.

Paperwork

Make sure that all papers are in order. At work, they should have you fill out tax forms so that you can be paid properly. You have a right to know when and how often you will be paid, and how much your hourly wage or salary will be. If you will be receiving any benefits, they should give you all materials about them and describe them to you in detail. At college, you should receive adequate notice of your official registration and the classes for which you have enrolled. Make sure that the grades your teachers give you match the ones that show up on your report card at the end of each semester, and that the proper number of credit hours are added to your record.

Additional Rights on the Job

Your employer should make very clear to you, whether verbally or on paper, what your responsibilities are on the job—this is your job description. Make sure that you know exactly what is expected of you. Also, the rules and regulations of the workplace should be made clear to you. Often you will get them on paper, or they will be posted somewhere at your place of employment. For example, if you are working at a restaurant, there may be rules posted about wearing all parts of a uniform and how to treat customers.

Additional Rights at College

You have a right to individual attention from your teachers, no matter how large your classes are or how busy they are. The needs of students should be a priority for them. If you need help, find out what your teachers' office hours are and visit them during those times. If you live at your college, you have a right to feel comfortable with your roommate. If you have any problem that you can't talk out together or with your resident assistant, you have the right to request a room transfer. You also have a right to extra help with your studies if you need it. Most colleges have tutoring and/or advising available.

Focusing on the Big Picture: Lifelong Learning

Although it seems as if everything comes to an end when you graduate high school, you are just beginning your life. You probably have three-quarters of your life left, much of which will be spent working, some of which will be spent studying and playing and thinking and dreaming. Whether you go on to college or to a full-time job, your learning doesn't stop when you step out of your high school doors for the last time as a student. Learning is a lifelong process. I am still learning all the time—about people, about my job, about writing, about what's happening in the world. There is too much to know just to stop taking it all in. If you continue to learn, you will grow as the world changes and your adaptability and flexibility will bring you success wherever you go.

I will close with the words of some of the people I interviewed, people who have all discovered that they continue to learn as they finish high school and continue on the paths that they have chosen for themselves.

NELSON CRUZ: "Just because you're street-smart and young, don't think you are the hippest person around."

BECKY AMATO: "Make a good academic reputation for yourself very early on in high school. Realize that when you do this, it can be very hard to keep up. But if you do earn a good name for yourself, and people know how well you can do, sometimes they give you extra leeway when you don't live up to expectations. Teachers who know you are usually a good student will cut you some slack when things sometimes get rough."

JAMES MORRIS: "Associate with people who have the same values as you do. And don't be worried if you don't have a lot of friends— just having a few who will be there for you is all that you need."

HEATHER POLLACK: "Get involved with something that you are very interested in. Don't be afraid or timid. Sometimes this can be studies, or extracurricular activitites, or even a job. My job selling popcorn at a movie theater launched my career in film—you never can tell what will happen to you!"

GWENAN WILBUR: "Try not to compare yourself to everyone else around you. Try to get a sense of what about yourself is good and true. Also, it isn't good to isolate yourself. Try to be involved with other people. And lastly, don't be afraid of being smart just because it isn't cool. Don't listen to adults who say that these are the best years of your life. Life gets better!"

DOMINIC CIRESI: "Have commitment and develop your personal skills as much as possible. When you commit yourself to something, have a reason for it and then just do it."

DEENA MOTTOLA: "Try not to focus entirely on grades—try to be well rounded, do creative things, be athletic. And every once in a while, do something wild (not illegal, just a bit crazy and different). If you make mistakes, you will learn from them and it will make you a more interesting person!"

GILBERT AGUILAR: "Balance your priorities and don't keep so much stress inside. Organized priorities are a way of showing that you take pride in yourself and what you are doing. Keeping your priorities balanced will help you to deal with the stress of everything and to accomplish what you want out of life."

CHRISTY WELLS: "People should make their own decisions and not always listen to other people. If I had done what other people thought I should do all the time, I would probably regret some of the decisions I made. Just do what you think is best."

LYDIA MOLINA: "No matter how much people say you can't be what you want, don't give up. All you have to do is show those people that you can achieve your goals."

SARAH LYMAN KRAVITS: "Try every activity that interests you. You never know how you will do at something, or how much you will like it, until you try. Even if you end up overextended, it doesn't matter. It's much easier to cut back on activities once you know which are your favorites than to convince yourself to try activities when you don't know what you will like. And get to know your teachers—you will learn so much more from them if they respect you as both a student and a friend."

DAVID ROWE: "The most important thing is to find out what really interests you and do it. It doesn't work to just 'follow the dollar' or pursue a career because everyone thinks you should. I also think it is very important to be persistent. I don't think it matters if you aren't a great student—or that you don't have a lot of money—you can still go to college, study abroad, do whatever you want. You just have to keep pushing and trying."

MELISSA REKAS: "The only way to get a lot out of life is to be your own person. It doesn't matter how you look or what you do—just be yourself. In middle school everyone tries to be the same, but in high school you can get a chance to develop a personality. Even if you think you are odd, there is always someone just as odd or even more strange than you."

REX RANDALL ERICKSON: "One, never give up. People who succeed aren't necessarily smarter or stronger or more popular than anyone else. They just don't give up, no matter how tough it is to continue.

"Two, everything happens for a reason. If there's anything I learned in my twenty-eight years, it's that when something bad happens, the first thing I do is look around for gold nuggets. So many times when something terrible happens, if I keep my wits about me and my eyes open, the situation ends up as good as or better than it would have anyway.

"Three, no problems are unique. Whenever I felt that my world was caving in around me, I would think about how many people there are on this earth, and how long people have been around, and I would realize that no problem I could ever have is worse than what people have suffered in the past. Broken hearts, bad grades, money woes, betrayed friends, legal problems—millions of people for thousands of years have had the same problems, and if they survived it, by God, so can I, and so can you."

The Difference You Make

As you think about your life and your choices over the next few years, remember that you are unique and special. By making the most out of who you are, you will create your own individual path in life. At the same time, you are also tied to those around you—you are an important part of the incredible tapestry of the human race. So embrace your experiences as you go—the good, the bad, and the ugly—they are all a part of life on this earth. But hold on to your vision of your life and of a better world; it will give you purpose and help you sense the deeper meaning of your life as you become an adult. Whatever you decide to do, whoever you choose to become, however you show the world your talents, believe in yourself and you will make a difference.

AFTERWORD

A few months before this book came out, Bill Clements died of cancer. He was a very special person to a lot of people in his family, his work life, and his community. I was fortunate enough to be able to work with Bill because he took responsibility for leading an organization called Lifeskills that I helped co-found a few years ago. We needed someone from the Tucson community who could marshal the energy and talents of others to focus on our public school system through this program, which brings people from all backgrounds and careers into high schools to tell students about what they do and how they got there. He, along with a woman named Shirley Kiser and a terrific staff and board of directors, made the program work by establishing it firmly within the community and education system.

Although Bill was only fifty-eight years old when he died, he contributed more than several lifetimes. At work, he was an interested, committed president and CEO of his company. As a leader in several philanthropic organizations, including Lifeskills, he took initiative, kept his word, and stuck his neck out to make improvements. As a friend he was caring and generous.

So why am I taking time to tell you about Bill? Two reasons. One is that Bill is an example of a life well lived—of a life that made the world better off for his having been part of it. The second is that even if you have never experienced a death of one of your family or friends, it is good to take stock of how precious life really is, how short our time here is (even for those who live to a ripe old age), and how much one individual life, like *yours* and like Bill's, can make a difference to so many people by creating so much good.

The greatest tribute I can pay to Bill is to carry on with the same energy, generous heart and spirit, and commitment to improve the world as he had. And I am asking you to do the same. It will make all the difference, to you personally and to those whose lives you touch.

APPENDIXES

APPENDIXES

Appendix A

Suggested Reading

Different people have different appetites for reading. Reading this book might be enough for you for a while, especially if you have a lot of reading for your classes. On the other hand, you might be hungry for more—more to read in general, or more information on a specific topic that came up in one of the chapters.

Here is a list to help you begin to explore what's available to you. It is by no means comprehensive! There are a great number of books out there that might mean something to you for one reason or another. Let this list be a guide to get you started on a lifetime adventure of reading. Books are listed according to topic and under each topic heading they are alphabetized by the author's last name (or publisher when no author is listed).

Self-Knowledge and Self-Esteem

Becoming the Me I Want to Be by Don Simmermacher (R & E Publishers, 1993). Information and exercises to help you build self-esteem, discover values, and set goals.

The Book of Questions by Gregory Stock, Ph.D. (Workman Publishers, 1987). A big long list of interesting questions dealing with all kinds of things—real life, relationships, values and ethics, decision-making, and more. Things to talk about in a group or to ask yourself in private. Get to know yourself better through questions.

Academic Help

Essential Vocabulary for College-Bound Students by Margaret Ann Haller (Prentice Hall, 1987). Vocabulary-building reading and exercises designed to help with tests like the SAT as well as with writing and reading at the college level.

Essentials of Writing by Vincent F. Hopper and Cedric Gale (Barron's, 1991). Workbook for improving English composition skills. Can be used alone or in conjunction with *Essentials of English,* by the same authors, which is a handbook of grammar and writing skills.

American Heritage Student Dictionary (Houghton Mifflin, 1994). This is just one example—any comprehensive dictionary will do. No one should be without one.

How to Solve Algebra Word Problems by William A. Nardi (Prentice Hall, 1987). Lots of practice and practical help with these—practice makes perfect.

Step-by-Step Guide to Correct English by Mary Ann Spencer Pulaski, Ph.D. (Prentice Hall, 1987). Helpful for writing college essays, term papers, essays for class, or anything that has to be "just right."

The High School Physics Tutor (Research and Educational Association [REA], 1993). This is actually six books—just replace *Physics* with any of the following: *Trigonometry, Biology, Chemistry, Algebra,* and *Geometry.* Each of the six volumes is a compilation of problems with complete solutions and explanations, ranging from the basic to the complex. A help with homework and with the basic concepts of any of these subjects.

The Elements of Style by William Strunk, Jr., and E. B. White (Macmillan, 3rd ed., 1979). A classic handbook on how to clarify and improve your writing. Talks about writing style, elements of composition, usage, and form, and commonly misused words and expressions.

Harmony—on Earth and in Relationships

50 Simple Things Kids Can Do to Recycle by The Earth Works Group (Earth Works Press, 1994). Helping to save your planet one piece at a time. Do your part!

Talking Justice: 602 Ways to Build and Promote Racial Harmony by Tamera Trotter and Joycelyn Allen (R & E Publishers, 1993). In response to the Los Angeles riots of 1992, these women came up with ideas and actions that, if practiced by each individual, can work to make us all more understanding, tolerant, and open-minded.

Potential Role Models

One of the best ways to learn about qualities such as commitment and motivation is to read about how other people turned those qualities into success. Any biography is great to read—find a person who means something to you. When you read a biography, you find out the details of how one person overcame obstacles, made decisions, and kept initiative going until goals were achieved. You might find some role models as you read. The four biographies below are just examples of what you might find interesting.

Thomas Edison: The Great American Inventor by Louise Egan (Barron's "Solutions" series, 1987).

Ella Fitzgerald by Bud Klimet (Chelsea House Publishers' "Black Americans of Achievement" series, 1988).

Martin Luther King, Jr.: Dreams for a Nation by Louise Quayle (Fawcett Columbine's "Great Lives" series, 1989).

Eleanor Roosevelt: A Life of Discovery by Russell Freedman (Clarion Books, 1993).

Physical and Mental Health

Too Old to Cry: Abused Teens in Today's America by Robert J. Ackerman, Ph.D., and Dee Graham (Tab Books, 1990). Although technically written for adults, this book gives a lot of useful information that is easy to read, and has quotes from teenagers throughout. A good resource if you are in a troubled situation—neglect, abuse, violence—and are trying to sort out what it is, what causes it, and what you can do about it.

Alcoholism: The Facts by Donald W. Goodwin (Oxford University Press, 1994). Basic facts regarding alcohol abuse—discusses the substance, the abuser, and those around who are also affected.

When Food's a Foe: How to Confront and Conquer Eating Disorders by Nancy J. Kolodny, M.A., M.S.W. (Little, Brown and Company, 1987). Straight facts and coping strategies for bulimia, anorexia, and compulsive overeating—what you do to yourself if you have an eating disorder and how to begin to change it.

What Do I Do Now? by Susan Kuklin (G. P. Putnam's Sons, 1991). Through telling the stories and using the quotes of real people, the author discusses the dilemmas and decisions surrounding teenage pregnancy.

Teenage Health Care by Gail B. Slap, M.D., and Martha M. Jablow (Pocket Books, 1991). This book is a great reference for information on both medical and social issues—growth and development, sports and nutrition, psychological and emotional issues, addictions, relationships, and more.

The Body Book: An Owner's Manual by Sara Stern (Workman Publishers, 1992). A fascinating look at everything your body is, does, and needs. Includes information on how the different systems work, how to keep yourself healthy, how substances affect you, emotions and relationships, and more.

Career Information and Advice

101 Great Answers to the Toughest Interview Questions by Ron Fry (Career Press, 1994). Can help you be prepared for whatever they might throw at you. Tons of possibilities with corresponding possible ways of answering.

Your Rights in the Workplace by Barbara Kate Repa (Nolo Press, 1994). Goes through your rights in detail regarding taking leave, hiring and firing, wages and hours, workers' compensation, discrimination, privacy, and more.

The Career Finder by Dr. Lester Schwartz and Irv Brechner (Ballantine Books, 1982). Starts with a questionnaire for you to answer about yourself to determine your Personal Career Profile, and then guides you through job descriptions of 1,500 entry-level jobs, showing you which might best suit you.

Working by Studs Terkel (Ballantine Books, 1974). A classic! The author interviews working people all over the country and records their comments in their own words. Good insights into diversity and the realities of the working world.

But What If I Don't Want to Go to College? by Harlow G. Unger (Facts on File, 1992). Alternative routes to success in mechanical and technical fields, transportation, the armed services, marketing and retail, health services, and others. Describes what kind of alternative education/training is needed, salary possibilities, job descriptions, other details.

College Help: School Reviews, Admissions, Success Strategies

Barron's Top 50: An Inside Look at America's Best Colleges (Barron's, 1993). Detailed reviews of top schools—their strengths and weaknesses, social and academic life, programs available, locations, lots of other details.

Majoring in the Rest of Your Life: Career Secrets for College Students by Carol Carter (Farrar, Straus & Giroux / Noonday, 1990). A how-to for success in college and beyond, with discussions of your talents and interests, goals, travel, careers, and how to focus your studies for a rewarding and successful professional life.

Making the Grade in College by Kenneth A. Green (Barron's, 1990). Practical information on managing your time, studying, dealing with the social life, and maximizing your use of the resources available to you.

ARCO's The Right College (Macmillan, 1994). Facts, figures, requirements, programs, financial aid information, etc., on more than 1,500 U.S. schools.

A Student's Guide to College Admissions: Everything Your Guidance Counselor Has No Time to Tell You by Harlow G. Unger (Facts on File, 1992). Just what it says! You don't always have time to see your counselor, and your counselor doesn't always have the time or the information that you need. This is a great reference you can turn to for answers to your important questions.

Appendix B

Clubs and Group Activities

Every high school is different and has a different smorgasbord of activity offerings for its students. The following list is to show you what could be out there; from here it is your job to find out what exactly takes place in your particular high school.

Team Sports

Keeping active is great for your health, and working with a group toward a common goal builds teamwork, commitment, cooperation, and dedication. Sometimes the competition may even end in victory, but whether or not that happens, you'll learn a lot. It doesn't matter what sport you play—find one that fits your schedule and your level/ area of athletic ability and give it a shot. Here is a list of possibilities:

- Baseball
- Basketball
- Cross-country
- Field hockey
- Football
- Golf
- Gymnastics
- Lacrosse
- Rugby
- Soccer
- Softball
- Swimming
- Tennis
- Track
- Volleyball
- Wrestling

Sport-related Physical Activities

As much as the players are sweating it out on the field, court, or track, some physical activity is happening on the sidelines as well. You can get some great exercise and coordination, not to mention having a lot of fun and developing a sense of belonging and some great friendships, with the following activities:

- Baton twirling
- Cheerleading
- Drill team/song leading/kick line
- Flag team/flag twirling

Sports Clubs and Other Physical Activities

Some sports or physical activities may not have a team, but you can still find an opportunity to participate in a club setting. Fun and physical exercise minus the competition.

- Aerobics
- Dance classes (ballet, jazz, modern, tap, folk, square, or country-western dancing)
- Hiking club
- Martial arts clubs (karate, tai kwon do, etc.)
- Running and/or walking
- Ski club
- Swim club
- Yoga and tai chi

Performing Arts

High school is a great time to hone your talents, no matter what area of the performing arts interests you. You will have a chance to learn technique and teamwork, develop your repertoire, and perform in front of others.

- Chorus
- Concert band
- Dance club
- Drama club
- Jazz ensemble
- Glee club

- Marching band
- Orchestra

Audio/Visual/Literary Arts

Whether you prefer to communicate with pictures or with words, there's a club or a publication that will help you expand your abilities and give you a chance to show what you do to others.

- Art club
- Literary magazine
- Radio station (on-air, production, or technical support)
- School newspaper
- Videographers' club
- Yearbook

Academic Teams

The spirit of competition thrives off the field as well. Pit your brain power against that of others and develop team spirit and cooperation in these activities.

- Chess team
- Competitive teams for shows such as "It's Academic"
- Debate team
- Math team

Language Clubs

These clubs give you a chance to expand your education beyond what you can do in class. You may practice for poetry readings or competitions, organize dinners featuring the foods of a particular country, make field trips to bookstores or restaurants, listen to music, have after-school-hours conversation opportunities, and more.

- French club
- German club
- Spanish club
- Clubs of any other languages taught at your school

Leadership

Do you want to be a leader? Do you want to have a say in decisions and make a difference? Student government, the governing board of your school class, or a military group may be the place for you. Offices such as president or vice president are won by election, so you'll have to convince your classmates you're the one for the job. Other positions may be available for those interested, such as members of the council for your class.

- Class councils/committees
- Individual class officers (president, vice president, secretary, treasurer)
- Junior ROTC or other military groups
- Student council/government
- Student representative to county board of education

Academic Enhancers

A lot of learning takes place after school, and clubs like these can enhance and supplement your daily classwork.

- Computer club—fun and educational activities to expand your computer knowledge
- Future Business Leaders of America (FBLA)—activities to promote business knowledge, such as the creation, advertising, and marketing of a product
- National Honor Society—members are chosen based on academic performance; organizes activities to promote academic success such as tutoring
- Science clubs—extensions of classroom activities in biology, chemistry, or other sciences
- Vocational/technical courses—after-school or half-day courses in trades such as automobile technology, cosmetology, and woodwork or metalwork

Hands-on

Activities are available in all sorts of areas for people who work well with their hands, whether they have artistic talents or a knack for mechanics. Students might do work within a club setting or float from group to group as others (teachers or students) need their expertise.

- Audio/visual mechanics (equipment repair, maintenance, and operation)
- Construction (floats for parades, in-school displays, outside signs, etc.)
- Mechanical drawing
- Scene construction for plays
- Sewing (costumes for dance or theatrical productions)
- Theatrical tech work (lights, sound, onstage scenery shift, special effects)
- Woodworking

Awareness and Self-Help

The world has its prejudices and its problems, and high school is a great time to begin to change and improve things for the better. You can have impact on your corner of the world as a high school student, and these clubs are some ways of going about it.

- Clubs for different ethnic groups—focus on the traditions and cultures of each group
- Cultural awareness club—focuses on knowledge about people different from ourselves and open-mindedness regarding those differences
- Ecology club—focuses on the health of the earth
- Students Against Drunk Driving (SADD)—promotes knowledge about driving drunk
- Students for Peace—works for peace and understanding among people
- Students Helping Other People (SHOP)—focuses on community service projects

If you feel as if a part of your *own* world is falling apart, there may be groups at school (often known as *student assistance programs*) that you can join to talk about it and find help from counselors and/or fellow students. For some students, school is the only strong community in their lives. This community can offer you some valuable support in the form of people who listen and offer advice instead of punishing you and putting you down. Whether you go to a group on your own or are referred by a friend or teacher because of trouble in school, you may find help.

Support groups may include:

- Conflict mediation/violence control/anger management
- Divorce, suicide, and self-esteem discussions
- Drug and alcohol abuse programs
- Grief groups
- Teenage pregnancy and parenthood groups

One more note: don't forget that there are a wealth of activities available to you *outside* your high school. It just takes a little more energy to seek them out and make time in your schedule to participate, but they are well worth it. Some centers will offer one particular activity (such as a dance school), others will offer everything from physical fitness to crafts to therapy groups to classes (such as a YMCA/YWCA/YMHA/YWHA might provide). Here is a basic list of what you might find in your community—there are sure to be more. A good place to look or call for a listing is your local community center or your public library.

- Boy Scouts
- Boy's State
- Camp Fire Girls
- Choirs for religious services
- Dance schools/companies
- 4H Club
- Future Farmers of America
- Girl Scouts
- Girl's State
- Language courses
- Painting classes
- Religious study through churches, synagogues, temples, or mosques
- Theater schools/companies
- YMCA/YWCA/YMHA/YWHA
- Youth groups

Appendix C

Scholarships, Awards, Grants, and Loans

The money is out there—it's just up to you to find it. One book estimates that since the 1970s more than $6.6 *billion* worth of scholarships have gone unclaimed. That's a lot of cash, and a lot of help! Also, not all scholarships require you to prove economical need—in fact, 80 percent of private-sector scholarships do not have need as a prerequisite. There are three kinds of help available to you as you prepare for further education:

Government

Loans and grants offered by federal or state governments; some need-based, some not; all require application.

Government funds available to you are divided into six categories, three of which are loans (which must be repaid), and three of which are grants (no repayment is necessary).

THE LOANS

- *Perkins Loans* are for full-time undergraduates and graduates who demonstrate exceptional financial need; the funds come from the school's allotment and the amount depends on what the school has available.
- *Stafford Loans* are for undergraduates and graduates enrolled at least half-time; available regardless of income, but the government pays the interest only on need-based loans; the funds come from the lender (bank or credit union), and the amount depends on length of enrollment and year in school.
- *Plus Loans* are for students who are still legal dependents of their parents and aren't based on income; the maximum award is cost of

education minus any other aid received; funds come from the lender (bank or credit union).

THE GRANTS

- *Pell Grants* are for undergraduates only and require financial need (calculated based on how much your family is able to contribute to the payment of your educational costs); amount depends in part on length of enrollment and year.
- *SEOG (Supplemental Educational Opportunity Grants)* are for undergraduates only and go only to those with exceptional financial need; the maximum is generally $4,000, depending on funds available at the school.
- *Work-Study* is for undergraduates and graduates both and provides jobs on or off campus; the amount earned cannot exceed demonstrated need; payment is by hour or salary, with all students paid at least monthly.

To be eligible even to apply for federal aid requires that you be a *U.S. citizen or eligible noncitizen*, have a *high school diploma or GED*, have a *Social Security number*, and make *satisfactory academic progress* at your studies. Whether you will receive aid, and how much, depends on a number of factors—the amount your chosen school is able to award, your family's financial situation, your student status, and your other sources of aid.

All of this information is a very brief summary of a government publication entitled *The Student Guide: Financial Aid from the U.S. Department of Education*, which can give you a much more comprehensive look at what you may be able to receive and how to apply for it. This booklet is updated every year and is available to you free. Sometimes your school, a counselor, or another organization will be able to give or lend you a copy. You can write to this address for information on how to obtain a copy of your own:

Federal Student Aid Information Center
P.O. Box 84
Washington, DC 20044

One other helpful publication: *Free Money for College from the Government* by Laurie Blum (Henry Holt, 1993). The author details all kinds of federal money—what it is, if you're eligible, and how to go about getting it.

College-based

Loans, grants, and scholarships offered by a college for students attending that college; some need-based, some not; some require application, some are awarded based on observation of performance at the school.

Listing all of the possibilities here would make this book three times as long as it is! There are tons of offerings out there—how many and what kind depend on the school you attend. Some you apply for, some you don't. Some are awarded based on academic success, some on athletic ability, some on status such as ethnic group or legacy (parent or relative attended the school), some on special talents or interests (such as the performing or visual arts), and some on financial need. They may come from the school's financial aid office, private scholarship funds, or a specific department of the school. Amounts can range from a few hundred dollars to the total cost of your education—tuition, room, board, even expenses.

Three paths of investigation are necessary for the student fund-hunter. *One: Talk to your guidance counselor.* Counselors are paid to know what's available to you. But they won't always have all the information. So try *two: Talk to the financial aid departments of any schools* to which you want to apply or have applied. And for a quick and comprehensive reference on all kinds of aid, all over the country, try *three: Visit your bookstore in the testing prep and college section.* One great book for college aid is called *Free Money from Colleges and Universities* by Laurie Blum (Henry Holt, 1993). The author details money available from a great many U.S. schools; she lists eligibility requirements, contact people and phone numbers, deadlines, dollar amounts, and other details for each scholarship or grant.

Private Sector

Loans, grants, and scholarships offered by private businesses and organizations; some need-based, some not; all students fulfilling individual eligibility requirements may apply.

This category has the largest number of different awards, ranging from checks from community associations to full scholarships awarded by national corporations. Eligibility requirements are all over the map. Your local Rotary Club may award scholarships for a high GPA; a local corporation may give an award to a student who shows promise in its line of business; national fraternities or sororities may award scholarships to high school students who have exemplified their ideals. Your most offbeat interests may be sources of income for your education!

Your best bet here, again, is the bookstore. Two books that have comprehensive, easy-to-understand listings are *The Scholarship Book* by Daniel J. Cassidy (Prentice Hall, 1993) and *Free Money for College* by Laurie Blum (Facts on File, 1994). Both list details for thousands of scholarships all over the country—locale, eligibility requirements, contact numbers and organizations, deadlines, amounts, and other facts and figures—and they index them by field of study/interest, eligibility requirements, and alphabetical order so that you can more easily find what applies to you. They also give tips on how to apply so as to give yourself the best chance of success.

If you intend to study abroad, Daniel J. Cassidy has also written *The International Scholarship Directory* (Career Press, 1993), which details scholarships available at schools around the globe.

The less you have to pay in college loans for the next couple of decades, the better! Taking the time to research now will pay off in both money and time saved; that way, once you are a member of the working world, your salary goes to your savings and your needs instead of just toward the repayment of loans. Most people are repaying loans of one kind or another at any given time, but try to avoid it as much as you can. Money is there for the taking if you can find it, apply for it, and win it. Go for it!

Do You Have Advice?

If you would like to give me your comments on what you did and didn't like about the book, I would greatly appreciate it. Or, if you have a story of your own which you think would illustrate an important point, please write it down on a separate sheet of paper. I'll use your comments and suggestions as I revise the book for future editions.

	YES	NO
1. This book changed the way I perceive myself and my future options.	—	—
2. I liked the various opinions and attitudes which the book reflects.	—	—
3. This book made me feel more comfortable about the future.	—	—
4. I would recommend this book to my friends.	—	—
5. On a separate sheet of paper, please give us your suggestions for improving this book.	—	—

6. I found out about this book by: (check one)
Seeing it in a bookstore ____
My teacher assigned it ____
It was a gift ____

Thanks for your suggestions. Mail the form to:
Carol Carter
Majoring in High School
Farrar, Straus and Giroux, Inc.
19 Union Square West
New York, NY 10003

Your name and address: _____

_____

_____

Phone: _____

	YES	NO
Do we have permission to quote you?	—	—
Do we have permission to contact you?	—	—